FOCUS ON THE FAMILY
R E S O U R C E S

Lead Your Teen
to a
Lifelong Faith

Joe White & Jim Weidmann, General Editors

TYNDALE

Tyndale House Publishers, Inc.
Wheaton, Illinois

Lead Your Teen to a Lifelong Faith

Copyright © 2005 by Focus on the Family
All rights reserved. International copyright secured.

A Focus on the Family book published by
Tyndale House Publishers, Wheaton, Illinois 60189

TYNDALE is a registered trademark of Tyndale House Publishers, Inc. Tyndale's quill logo is a trademark of Tyndale House Publishers, Inc.

All Scripture quotations, unless otherwise indicated, are taken from the *Holy Bible, New International Version* ®. NIV ®. Copyright © 1973, 1978, 1984 by the International Bible Society. Used by permission of Zondervan Publishing House. All rights reserved. Scripture quotations marked NKJV are taken from the *New King James Version*. Copyright © 1982 by Thomas Nelson, Inc. Used by permission. All rights reserved.

Based on the *Parents' Guide to the Spiritual Mentoring of Teens* (Focus on the Family/Tyndale House Publishers, 2001)

Contributing writers:

John Duckworth	Bob Waliszewski
Larry Weeden	Chuck Johnson
Joe White	Lissa Halls Johnson
Andy Braner	Jim Weidmann
Keith Wall	Bob Smithouser

Cover Design: Lauren Swihart
Cover Photography: Photodisc
Cover Copy: Carol Hubbard

The use of material from various Web sites does not imply endorsement of those sites in their entirety.

Focus on the Family books are available at special quantity discounts when purchased in bulk by corporations, organizations, churches, or groups. Special imprints, messages, and excerpts can be produced to meet your needs. For more information, contact: Focus on the Family, 8605 Explorer Drive, Colorado Springs, CO 80920; or phone (800) 932-9123.

ISBN 1-58997-084-5
Printed in the United States of America

05 06 07 08 09 10 / 10 9 8 7 6 5 4 3 2 1

Contents

Part 4: Discipling Day by Day

How to Use This Book

It's great to have a teenager. In fact, while your child's teen years can be among the most challenging you'll face as a parent, they can also be the best years of your parenting life.

For one thing, raising a teenager will give new depth and fervency to your prayer life! You're likely to be reminded every day that by yourself, you're not up to the task. That's okay; it means you're just like the rest of us.

Passing the baton of faith successfully to your teen will, at the end of the process, give you a tremendous sense of victory and satisfaction. "We did it! We did it!" you'll want to shout.

Parenting your teen, especially in the area of spiritual growth, is a divine calling, a challenge that will demand the best you've got to give, and a wonderful privilege. In this book, based on the *Parents' Guide to the Spiritual Mentoring of Teens* (Focus on the Family/Tyndale 2001), you'll find practical, parent-tested advice to guide you each step of the way:

- You'll see that no matter what your situation, and no matter how good a job you have or haven't done so far, you can be the effective mentor your child needs.
- You'll gain a clear understanding of the fundamental change that takes place in the parent-child relationship during the teen years, and of what that means for influencing your teen's faith.
- You'll learn that the key to mentoring your teen is a great relationship, and acquire crucial insights into building and maintaining that bond.
- You'll discover ways in which to disciple your teen, allowing you to tailor a plan to fit your family.

Mentoring your teen is a challenge, but one you face with the Lord of heaven at your side. He loves you, He loves your child, and He is committed to your success.

As He encouraged Joshua, who faced the daunting job of leading Israel into the Promised Land, so He encourages you: "Be strong and courageous. Do not be terrified; do not be discouraged, for the LORD your God will be with you wherever you go" (Joshua 1:9).

Studying with a Group

Working your way through this book with fellow parents—whether in a small group, Sunday school class, retreat, or other setting—is a great idea. You'll be fortified by the insights and support they offer.

Want to study all the chapters in 16 weeks? Feel free! If you prefer shorter courses, try tackling the book in four segments of four weeks each.

In each session you'll find the following:

Startup—An introduction to get you thinking about the topic.

Survey—A chance to assess where you are on the subject, and even to have a few well-deserved laughs.

Scripture—Biblical input to read and wrestle with.

Strategies—Down-to-earth suggestions for everyday mentoring.

Steps to Take—Ways to turn your good intentions into action.

The guide in the back of this book will help your leader make the most of your time together. That works best if you've read and completed each interactive chapter before the group meets. You'll find the advice, questions, and planning tools well worth your effort.

Studying on Your Own

You don't have to join a group to benefit from this book. You—or you and your spouse—can complete each chapter individually or in tandem, at your own pace. If you're studying with a spouse, talk about your survey answers. Plan your action steps together. Pray together for your teen, and for the wisdom and stamina God wants to give you.

If you're working through this book alone, remember that you aren't *really* alone. God's Spirit can be your teacher and counselor—and, if you like, you can enlist a friend to be a sounding board and keep you honest.

Whether you soak up these insights in a group or on your own, we encourage you to get a copy of the *Parents' Guide to the Spiritual Mentoring of Teens*. This nearly 600-page reference book is packed with plenty of advice we couldn't include in this one; you'll want to have it handy to help you meet even more of the challenges of passing the baton of faith to your sometimes perplexing, always priceless teen.

PART 1

Becoming Your Teen's Spiritual Coach

1

What Mentors Are Meant For

startup

Remember when your teenager was a baby?

You probably took care of that child's every need. You bathed, fed, dressed, and changed her. Later you screened her friends, signed her up for ballet lessons or basketball, and told her when to practice the flute or feed the dog. You were still in control, more or less.

Those were the good old days, right?

A lot of parents wish the adolescent years were just a continuation of the preteen process. They'd like to control everything their teen does.

As you may have noticed, few teenagers share that view.

It's only normal: As the young person's need to take on greater responsibility increases, it's vital that the "control center" begins to move from parent to offspring.

That's where mentoring comes in.

Being a mentor is like being a coach. When would-be athletes are young, a coach begins with the basics. He explains everything. He's not just on the field—he's positioning kids' feet and arms, showing them how to catch the pass or hit the ball.

When the day finally arrives for a real game, though, the coach stays on the sidelines. The players take the field. It's the same way with parents who want to be spiritual mentors.

In the early years, we may show our children how to pray, even giving them words to say and telling them to close their eyes. But eventually our kids are praying on their own. We might wish we could elbow our way into those conversations, but all we can do is make suggestions from the sidelines.

Our halftime pep talks may be delivered on a weekend or during a family vacation. Our post-game analyses may occur at bedtime or over pie at a coffee shop.

Sometimes we'll find ourselves sharing the coaching duties with others—camp counselors, youth leaders, or Sunday school teachers. But because we're the parents of our teens, we'll be their "head coaches"—their primary mentors, for better or for worse.

We hope this chapter helps make it for the better.

survey

1. When you hear the word "mentor," which of the following comes to mind?
   a. An alien with a huge brain
   b. A tin of powerful breath mints
   c. A wise old man who keeps calling you "Grasshopper"
   d. Other _____

2. **When it comes to spiritually mentoring your teen, what have you tried so far?**
   a. Nothing
   b. Memorizing books of the Bible that start with "Q"
   c. Showing how to multiply loaves and fishes
   d. Other _____

3. **Which of the following best describes your mentoring style?**
   a. Coach
   b. Disinterested Bystander
   c. Benevolent Despot
   d. Other _____

4. **Walking alongside your teen rather than controlling him would be**
   a. A tremendous relief
   b. An abdication of my responsibility
   c. The worst idea since Low-Carb Superglue
   d. Other _____

5. **By the time you're done with this book, you hope to**
   a. See spiritual progress in your teenager
   b. Feel more confident in guiding your teen's spiritual growth
   c. Learn how to work the remote on your DVD player
   d. Other _____

scripture

1. Read Proverbs 1:8-9. Based on this passage, would you say that mentoring is a job for dads only? Why or why not?

Why do you suppose King Solomon bothered to explain why his son should listen to his parents' spiritual guidance? Why not just order the son to listen?

2. Look at Proverbs 3:1-3. What two reasons does Solomon give for following his instructions?

If mentoring your teen will bring him or her the same benefits, is it worth your effort? Why or why not?

3. Read Proverbs 4:1-6. What kind of mentor does Solomon's father, David, sound like?

How do you think two key events in David's life—standing up to Goliath and having an adulterous affair with Bathsheba—may have affected the way he mentored Solomon?

What's one positive spiritual event in your life that you could use as an example when you mentor your teen?

What's one spiritual mistake you've made that your teen could learn from?

strategies

What does a mentor look like? These students recall what their "coaches" did to guide them:

- "My mother would kneel beside my bed at night and pray for me before telling me good night. It was often during the prayers that she was able to communicate her feelings or concerns to me. She also told me this often and wrote it down for me: 'I have great worth apart from my performance because Christ gave His life for me and therefore imparted great value to me. I am deeply loved, fully pleasing, totally forgiven, accepted, and complete in Christ Jesus.'"
- "My dad always made me go to sports practices when I didn't want to because he said I have to keep my commitments. This caused a lot of yelling, but I learned something very important about commitments."
- "When we were little, my mom read us Bible stories either after dinner or before we went to bed. Her way of making sure we were listening was to ask us questions about the story."

Mentoring takes many forms. But the purpose is the same: to help your child develop a solid faith of his or her own.

It's All in the Timing

As your child matures, he needs you less as a governor and more as a mentor—someone who leads by walking alongside.

Mentors major in guiding, encouraging, teaching—not controlling. The transition from governor to mentor is made by slowly letting go during the teen years, giving more and more free rein as the child proves himself trustworthy.

Instead of maintaining a viselike grip on the youngster's life until the last possible second when he leaves home, the wise parent shifts responsibility and choices a bit at a time, a little more each year.

Making the transition from governor to mentor requires courage—as all battles do. And timing is crucial.

The parents of 13-year-old Derek, for example, know that he's ready to take on more responsibility for his own spiritual growth. He's so zealous, in fact, that kids at school call him "Bible boy." He even started an after-school prayer meeting in a classroom. Now's the time for Derek's folks to offer him a new challenge—a missions trip during spring break, perhaps, or a backyard Bible club for neighborhood kids in the summer.

By contrast, 15-year-old Brianna has always been more interested in surfing the Web than in searching the Scriptures. Her parents are helping her find Web sites that offer devotional readings, in the hope that she'll develop the habit of spending "quiet times" with God.

It wouldn't make sense for "Bible boy" Derek's parents to hover over his devotional life, planning his next 365 readings by chapter and verse and sitting on the edge of his bed to make sure he doesn't miss one. He's past that point. Nor would it be wise for webmistress Brianna's folks to simply hope that her disinterest in Bible reading will somehow take care of itself. Demanding that Brianna muscle her way through Leviticus might foster only resentment and failure, but starting with her Internet enthusiasm just may work.

The parents of Derek and Brianna know these things because they understand that mentors must be clear-eyed observers of their kids. As Dr. James Dobson has written, "It is a wise mother or father who can let go little by little as the growing child is able to stand on his or her own. If you watch and listen carefully, the critical milestones will be obvious."[1]

The Mentor's Job Description

To better understand what a mentor does, let's consider two fictional stories about those who led by walking alongside.

In *The Lord of the Rings* trilogy by J. R. R. Tolkein, Gandalf is mentor to Bilbo Baggins. Gandalf doesn't make Bilbo's journey for him; he imparts wisdom, practical advice, and skill so that Bilbo can complete his own quest.

In the film *Karate Kid,* Mr. Miyagi is Daniel's mentor, teaching him how to control his temper, be strong, and deal with bullies. The martial-arts master doesn't fight Daniel's battles for him; he cultivates the boy's self-discipline, preparing Daniel to face enemies on his own turf.

In the real-life story of your teen, he or she is the hero on a journey. Yours is the role of mentor.

If you aren't a perfect mentor, join the club. In fiction and in life, most mentors are flawed. Fortunately, imperfections—and your admissions of them—can make your teen more open to your guidance. And if you've learned from your mistakes, you have road-tested wisdom to offer the hero in your home.

This doesn't mean, of course, that your teen will always be eager to hear that wisdom. Even fictional mentors are often resented and their advice resisted—until the hero learns the hard way that Yoda or Mom or Dad was right.

The Mentor as Model

Mentors are role models, too.

Imagine Obi-Wan Kenobi, mentor to Luke Skywalker in the original *Star Wars* movie, trying to train his aspiring Jedi knight as follows:

Obi-Wan: Use the Force, Luke.

Luke: Why?

Obi-Wan: Uh . . . I'm not sure. Never used it. I hear it's very effective, though.

Luke: But—

> *Obi-Wan:*   Now, about this light saber. To turn it on, you just push this button. No, that's not it. Maybe this switch over here . . .
>
> *Luke:*   Haven't you used that, either?
>
> *Obi-Wan:*   Hey, smart mouth! What do you think you are, a Jedi master? You kids today! Why, when I was your age . . .

Mentors aren't perfect, but they need to practice what they preach. In fact, they may have to practice a *lot* before they offer advice to their apprentices.

Tracy, 16, receives frequent lectures about her "bad attitude" toward the church youth group. Yet every Sunday in the car, she watches her mother stage a post-service "roast" of their pastor, the committee that chooses music, and the elders who draw up the church budget. Will Tracy change her attitude? Probably not for the better.

Being a role model may be an intimidating assignment, but it's ours nonetheless. Whether we want them to or not, our teens are watching. Regardless of our words, they'll try behavior that seems to work for us. They're telling us, in effect, "Mom and Dad, who you are and what you do speak so loudly that I can't hear what you're saying."

If that makes you feel more like a muddle than a model, there's hope.

God uses imperfect models, too.

Still, we're easier to use when we've practiced enough to know which end of the light saber is up.

Mentoring: The Wave of Your Future

Like it or not, your relationship with your young person is changing—and *must* change. You can't influence your teen in the way you did when he or she was younger.

But you *can* choose to work *with* the process and not against it. That's why the most successful parents of teenagers will:

1. Recognize the change.
2. Accept the change.
3. Plan accordingly—gradually transferring control and responsibility for choices and actions to their teens.

steps to take

1. Are you acting as your teen's governor—or mentor? Look at each of the following pairs of statements. Circle a dot between the two statements to show where you are on the spectrum between governor and mentor.

GOVERNOR		MENTOR
a. You tend to fight your teen's battles for him	•••••	You try to arm him with the weapons of truth and character to face his own foes
b. You try to control your teen's choices	•••••	You give her the facts she needs to make her own decisions
c. You tend to pretend that your teen hasn't grown	•••••	You watch for milestones that show he's ready for more independence
d. You only give advice about the future	•••••	You try to help him deal with his fears about the future
e. You tend to lecture out of frustration	••••••	You try to offer motivation and inspiration when she's open to it

GOVERNOR		MENTOR

f. You tend to deal only • • • • • You try to plant
with crises of the values that will be
moment useful to him later

g. You pressure your teen • • • • • You try to help her be
to conform outwardly transformed inwardly
to your expectations through personal
interaction with God

Now mark an "X" on each line of dots to show where
you'd *like* to be a month from now.

In those areas where you'd like to change, which of the
following do you think might be holding you back?
a. Fear that your teen might hurt himself or herself
b. Not knowing what to do
c. Feeling too busy
d. Being too tired
e. Being too impatient
f. Other _____

Based on your answer to the previous question, which of
the following do you most need to ask God for this week?
a. Courage
b. Wisdom
c. Time
d. Energy
e. Patience
f. Other _____

2. One part of mentoring is being a role model. On a scale of
1 to 10 (1 being horrified, 10 being ecstatic), circle a number to show how happy you'd be if your son or daughter
imitated your habits in each of the following areas:

HANDLING ANGER   1 2 3 4 5 6 7 8 9 10

GAMBLING   1 2 3 4 5 6 7 8 9 10

DRIVING   1 2 3 4 5 6 7 8 9 10

ALCOHOL USE   1 2 3 4 5 6 7 8 9 10

SEXUAL BEHAVIOR   1 2 3 4 5 6 7 8 9 10

DRESS   1 2 3 4 5 6 7 8 9 10

WORK HOURS   1 2 3 4 5 6 7 8 9 10

CREDIT CARD DEBT   1 2 3 4 5 6 7 8 9 10

3. Now ask yourself about behaviors you *want* your teen to imitate. In each of the following areas, try to name an action you've taken in the last six months. Then indicate whether your teen knows about it. (Note: If you're thinking that performing good deeds in front of others in order to win their praise is hypocritical, you're right [Matthew 6:1-6]. But the point of letting your teen see these actions is to teach him or her to follow in your footsteps.)

SHARING YOUR FAITH
An action you took:

Does your teen know about it? ___ YES   ___ NO

SHOWING HOSPITALITY
An action you took:

Does your teen know about it? ___ YES   ___ NO

FORGIVING
An action you took:

Does your teen know about it? ___ YES   ___ NO

EXERCISING SELF-CONTROL
An action you took:

Does your teen know about it? ___ YES ___ NO

GIVING GENEROUSLY
An action you took:

Does your teen know about it? ___ YES ___ NO

RESPONDING TO THE NEEDS OF THE POOR
An action you took:

Does your teen know about it? ___ YES ___ NO

SUPPORTING MISSIONARIES
An action you took:

Does your teen know about it? ___ YES ___ NO

PRAYING
An action you took:

Does your teen know about it? ___ YES ___ NO

Based on your answers, which of the following do you
need to work on more?
a. Putting your faith into action
b. Letting your teen see you acting on your faith

4. When it comes to guiding your teenager spiritually, do you fear you have nothing to share? Maybe you're not as unqualified as you think.

What's one aspect of the Christian life that you know a *little* more about than your teen does?

What's a spiritual mistake you've made that your teen hasn't made yet?

What did you learn from it that you could pass on to your teen?

Have you made even a *tiny* bit of progress since beginning your relationship with God?

If so, what could you tell your teen about that?

2

You Can Do It!

startup

If you're like most parents of teens, the biggest question on your mind as you consider being a spiritual mentor to your child is probably, "Can I really do this?" Or you may have already concluded, "I'm not cut out for this!"

Fueling those doubts may be thoughts like these:

- "My child is already 17 and will be gone in a year. It's too late for us to get started now."

- "I'm a single parent, or I'm married but going it alone spiritually because of my spouse's lack of interest. I just don't have the resources (time, energy, money) for the job."

- "I've blown it with my child in the past, leaving our relationship in a shambles. He's not about to start listening to me now."

- "My parents didn't do a good job of training me spiritually. I don't even know where to begin with my own child."

- "I made sure my child was taught well in her younger years. There's not much more I can do now, when she seems to listen to her friends more than she does to me."
- "I'm far from being a model Christian myself. If I try to start mentoring my child spiritually, he'll blow me off as a hypocrite."

If you relate to one or more of those concerns, you've got a lot of company. There probably isn't a Christian parent alive who doesn't feel inadequate in at least one of those areas.

But it's also true that millions of parents are exerting a positive influence on their teens' spiritual development every day. You can, too.

survey

1. **When you were a teen, who was the closest thing you had to a spiritual mentor?**
   a. Your mother
   b. Your father
   c. Dick Clark on *American Bandstand*
   d. Other _____

2. **What part of your spiritual journey as a teen would you like your teenager to experience, too?**
   a. Warm fellowship around the campfire
   b. A missions trip
   c. Being terrified by midnight showings of movies about the end times
   d. Other _____

3. **What's your biggest fear about spiritually mentoring your teen?**
   a. That you've waited too long to start
   b. That she'll reject your attempts to guide her

   c. That he'll turn into a spiritual giant and you won't
     be able to find shoes the right size
   d. Other _____

4. **When it comes to being a role model for your teen, you**
   a. Put Mother Teresa to shame
   b. Might be slightly better than Freddy Krueger
   c. Hope to be out of town for the next six years
   d. Other _____

5. **If mentoring a teen is like passing a baton in a relay race, then**
   a. You've already dropped the baton
   b. Your teen doesn't want the baton
   c. You'd rather try the javelin throw
   d. Other _____

scripture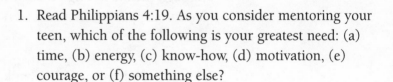

1. Read Philippians 4:19. As you consider mentoring your teen, which of the following is your greatest need: (a) time, (b) energy, (c) know-how, (d) motivation, (e) courage, or (f) something else?

   Do you believe God can meet that need? Why or why not?

2. Check out James 1:5. In which of the following areas do you most need wisdom: (a) resolving conflict with your teen, (b) knowing how to make spiritual things sound less "boring," (c) being firm without being overbearing, (d) knowing which things to teach first, or (e) something else?

Have you asked God for wisdom in that area? If so, what happened? If not, why not?

3. Look up 2 Corinthians 12:9-10. When it comes to spiritual mentoring, what's your greatest weakness?

   Do you believe God has the power to compensate for that weakness? Why or why not?

4. Read Isaiah 40:30-31. What part of spiritual mentoring sounds most exhausting to you?

   What do you think it means to "hope in the Lord"?

   Are you ready to depend on God's strength to get you through the mentoring process? If not, what would have to happen before you'd be ready?

5. Consider Philippians 1:6. What kind of "good work" has God started in your teen's life so far?

   What kind of person do you hope your teen will be when that work is completed?

   If God is calling you to be a mentor to your teen, can you trust Him to complete that process, too? Why or why not?

6. If you had to choose one of the previous verses as your "spiritual mentoring motto," which would it be? Why?

strategies

Afraid you can't mentor your teen? Let's consider six common concerns that make parents feel inadequate.

Concern #1: Too Late to Start

Perhaps you've never been very intentional about your child's spiritual training. Now he's 16 or 18. Haven't you missed your opportunity?

Even in only a year, or just a few months, you can make an eternal difference.

If your teen is beginning her senior year of high school, for example, and you start today to invest yourself daily in her spiritual growth, you can share at least 365 great and potentially life-changing experiences.

Even if you have only 30 days before your child goes to college or joins the military, that's long enough to help him establish the habit of making time to meet with God every day.

Starting late doesn't mean you've got to spend an hour a day feeding the Bible to your teen (which isn't going to happen anyway). Just 10 minutes a day can plant a love for Him and His Word deep in your teen's heart.

Concern #2: Going It Alone

Yes, your load will be greater than if you had a spouse to help carry it. But here are some encouraging things to remember:

1. You're not really alone. God is on your team; He cares even more about the spiritual growth of your teen than you do. People in your local church and community are almost certainly willing to help as well. They need to be asked; they probably won't approach you and volunteer.

2. You can connect your teen with Christian role models who partially "replace" your missing spouse. Since most single parents are moms, this usually means finding strong male role models. Seek out a youth leader, teacher, coach, camp counselor, or other reliable man who cares about teens and is willing to become involved.

3. As hectic and demanding as your life may be, you can follow the example of other single parents who grab a few minutes at breakfast or bedtime to open the Bible and pray with their kids; who use times in the car and elsewhere to talk about what's happening in the child's life and apply biblical principles; who include in their teen's sack lunch a note that says, "I love you and God loves you." Consistent planting and watering of the smallest seeds can yield a big harvest of faith.

Concern #3: Blew It in the Past

Perhaps you were an absentee parent, emotionally if not physically; you were ruled by anger that hurt your child and destroyed the relationship; you struggled with an addictive behavior that caused your child to lose respect for you; or you tried to force-feed your faith to your child, and now he wants nothing to do with Christianity.

Relationships can be rebuilt. Begin with prayer, confessing your mistakes to God. Then ask Him to open your child's mind and heart, heal the hurts, and give you wisdom, grace, and love for the task.

Next, go to your child and admit that you blew it. Be specific about what you did wrong. Forgiving you may take time and hard emotional and spiritual work. Be patient; continue to show your teen day by day that you're serious about overcoming past mistakes and becoming a better, more godly parent.

If the relationship is so damaged that no amount of effort seems capable of restoring it, seek help from a qualified Christian counselor.

Concern #4: Own Parents Didn't Mentor Well

Your parents' shortcomings in this area don't mean you can't succeed with your own child. You're not doomed to repeat their mistakes.

Would you be better off if the priority and methods of spiritual mentoring were already ingrained in your mind through having received them from your own mom and dad? Would that have given you a head start? Of course. But if you want to learn how to mentor your teen in spite of your background, you can and you will—through this course, for instance.

What if your experience with spiritual mentoring wasn't just poor but actually painful? Do you have to get healthy emotionally before you can begin to mentor your own teen? No. We all carry hurts from the past, but we can choose to move ahead in spite of them.

If you have such hurts, by all means seek help. But resolve that your past will not keep you from being an effective mentor to your own child.

Concern #5: Already Done All I Can

Some Christian parents feel that, having raised their children in church, they've finished the job. Others are content to leave the training of their teens to "experts"—the youth pastor or a parachurch group. Still others, considering the powerful influence of peers and the culture, just throw up their hands in despair.

If you think your role in the spiritual training of your teenager is over, think again. Now is not the time to coast.

There's still the fourth quarter to play. No matter how well you've done up to this point, this is the period when the game is won or lost.

The fourth quarter is the time when the opponent is more determined than ever. Peers are speaking the loudest. Hollywood is offering its most appealing and misleading enticements. Our "anything goes" culture is pressing home its most convincing arguments.

The final quarter of your parenting career can be your finest hour—or the time when you see everything you've worked for come undone. Keep working all the way to the last tick of that game clock.

Concern #6: Not a Good Example

True, you can't give your child what you don't have; you can't expect him to grow above your own level of spiritual maturity. You need to have such a faith yourself, and to live it out in front of your child day by day.

But you don't have to be a perfect Christian to be a good role model. You don't even have to pretend. Your teen will respect and trust you more if you're honest about your shortcomings.

Don't forget that you can grow *with* your child, too. Becoming more like Jesus Christ every day can be a shared journey.

Finally, remember that you don't have to be the only positive influence in your teen's life. There may be other people—your spouse, a grandparent, a pastor, a teacher. Most importantly there is God, who works without ceasing to draw and guide and nurture your child. He will never give up shaping her into the image of Jesus Christ (see Romans 8:29).

God Has Made You Adequate

As you face the prospect of serving as a spiritual mentor to your teen, it's easy to feel inadequate for the task. If you find yourself feeling like that, congratulations! You're right where God wants you.

Only those who know they can't do it on their own turn to Him for help.

steps to take

1. If you're afraid that it's too late to start mentoring your teen, please answer the following.

   Approximately how many days are left until your teen graduates from high school?

   If you had to choose three things to accomplish in that time, which of the following would they be?
   a. Helping your teen establish the habit of regular prayer and Bible reading
   b. Showing him or her why the Bible is reliable
   c. Getting your teen to memorize a dozen key passages of Scripture
   d. Making sure he or she has a personal relationship with Christ
   e. Getting him or her to meet the needs of other people
   f. Other _____

   If you had to choose just two of those things to accomplish, which would they be?

   If you had to choose just one of them, which would it be?

2. If you feel alone in the mentoring process, please answer the following:

What are two things you've accomplished without the help of a spouse?

Which of the following is hardest for you to provide?
a. A male or female role model
b. Understanding your teen's needs as a male or female
c. Enough attention to your teen, because you have to do everything yourself
d. Money to pay for things like missions trips and Christian concerts
e. Emotional support, since you've got issues of your own

Which of the following are you willing to ask a leader at your church about?
a. Finding a volunteer to spend time with your teen
b. Borrowing books that could help you understand your teen's needs
c. Help with chores like doing your taxes and changing your car's oil
d. Financial aid like camp scholarships
e. Referral to a counselor to talk through your own problems

3. If you think you blew it with your teen in the past, please complete the following.

Next to each of the following steps, write a "D" if you've already done it—or an "N" if it's a step you need to take. Then circle the "N" step you need to take first.
___ Believe the relationship can be rebuilt
___ Confess your mistakes to God
___ Ask God to open your teen's mind and heart, heal

the hurts, and give you wisdom, grace, and love for the task

___ Admit to your teen that you blew it, being specific about what you did wrong

___ Show your teen day by day that you're serious about overcoming past mistakes

___ If necessary, seek help from a qualified Christian counselor

4. If your own parents didn't mentor you well, please answer the following.

Which of the following did your own parents *not* teach you?
a. How to balance your checkbook
b. How to get through childbirth
c. How to do your job
d. How to use a computer

Which of these things have you managed to do anyway?

Which of the following resources could help you learn how to mentor?
a. This course
b. Other books
c. Parents at church who've raised teens
d. Your youth pastor
e. Trial and error
f. The Holy Spirit

5. If you assume you've already done all you can to mentor your teen, please complete the following.

Mark "T" or "F" for each statement to indicate whether it's true or false.

___ Your teen is 100 percent ready to enter the adult world and keep his or her faith intact

___ Your teen literally refuses to listen to anything you say

___ Your teen can't be negatively influenced by peers, the media, or teachers

___ God has given you special permission to quit parenting

If you marked "F" by any of the statements, what does that tell you about whether you're done guiding your young person?

6. If you fear you'd be a poor role model for your teen, please answer the following.

Which of these is true of you?
a. You're not a Christian
b. You're not perfect
c. You're okay, but nothing to write home about
d. You're perfect, just too humble

Which of the following will you do this week?
a. Be honest with your teen about your shortcomings in the area of _____
b. Hold up Jesus as a better example of _____
c. Ask your teen to grow with you in the area of

_____

3

The Goal of Spiritual Training

startup

Your high school senior is about to graduate.

You're sitting in the auditorium as your teenager, looking proud yet awkward in his or her cap and gown, chats and laughs with friends while you wait for the ceremony to begin.

The school band gets ready to work its shaky way through endless replays of "Pomp and Circumstance" as the graduates walk across the stage to receive their diplomas. Around you, people are talking and waving; parents with video cameras are setting up, preparing to capture every priceless moment.

Watching your child, you experience a flood of memories and emotions, a mixture of happiness and pride. You enjoy reminiscing for a few minutes.

Then your thoughts turn to the future, to the hopes and dreams you hold for your child. You wonder whether your teen is really prepared to take on a world—at college or in the workplace—that will be hostile to his or her faith and values. The corners of your mouth turn down, and worry lines crease your forehead.

Will your teenager be ready? Will his or her faith in God and relationship with Him be strong enough to stand up to the challenges that are coming?

You can start now to help ensure that when that day comes, the answer will be yes.

Instilling that kind of faith in your child is a Christian parent's most important responsibility. But just what does that kind of faith look like?

As with any target you hope to hit, you need to know what you're aiming at if you're to have the best chance of achieving success. That's what this session is about.

survey

1. Spiritually speaking, which of the following comes closest to the person you hope your teen will become?
   a. Billy Graham
   b. Billy Sunday
   c. Billy Bob Thornton
   d. Other _____

2. **Your teen knows the Bible as well as he knows**
   a. The back of his hand
   b. The back of his head
   c. The Urdu translation of the Periodic Table of Elements
   d. Other _____

3. **Which of the following service projects do you most wish your teen would undertake?**
   a. Building an orphanage in Guatemala
   b. Visiting a nursing home
   c. Picking the crushed Doritos out of the carpet in his room
   d. Other _____

4. **Your teen's worldview could be expressed in the words,**
   a. "The chief aim of man is to glorify God and enjoy Him forever."
   b. "I love you, you love me, we're a happy family."
   c. "Can we get cable?"
   d. Other _____

5. **If you could start over with spiritually mentoring your child, you would**
   a. Set higher goals
   b. Set more realistic goals
   c. Hire Joe White to live in your basement
   d. Other _____

scripture

Each of the following passages hints at one or more goals God has for every believer—including your teen. After each passage, list all the goals you can find.

1. The passage: Romans 8:29. The goal(s):

2. The passage: Ephesians 1:10. The goal(s):

3. The passage: Acts 17:11. The goal(s):

4. The passage: Philippians 3:10-11. The goal(s):

5. The passage: Matthew 22:34-40. The goal(s):

6. The passage: Galatians 5:22-23. The goal(s):

7. The passage: Micah 6:8. The goal(s):

strategies

When it comes to being a spiritual mentor to your teen, what targets are worth all the effort it will take to hit the bull's-eye?

Target #1: A Personal, Vibrant Relationship with Jesus Christ

Our teens need to leave home having a personal relationship with Jesus Christ. That means it's real to them, and it's theirs.

If a child has grown up in a Christian home, gone to church and Sunday school and youth group all his life, maybe even attended a Christian school, it's easy to assume that at some point he placed his faith in Christ. We want to believe that he loves God and seeks to follow biblical principles.

The fact is, however, that many such children haven't truly or fully committed their lives to Christ; they feel free to follow biblical principles *or not* depending on the situation.

We can't take a teen's faith for granted. By probing gently with questions, and by observing the daily choices that make up his lifestyle, we can get an idea of how real his faith is to him.

Sixteen-year-old Nikki had trusted in Jesus as her Savior at the age of nine. But she grew up with the view that the Christian life consists mostly of trying to follow rules. She recalls, "It never occurred to me that God wanted a close relationship with me, that He wanted me to know Him and love Him as a friend and Father. When I read the Bible at all, which wasn't often, it was out of a sense of duty rather than any sense of wanting to do it for myself or of expecting Him to reveal Himself to me."

Most people would have thought Nikki was a "good Christian." But a closer look and a candid conversation would have revealed that she was only going through the motions.

Our goal is to send off a high school graduate who, with all her heart, mind, soul, and strength, loves God and wants to know and serve Him better because of that overflowing love. That's the essence of the Christian life, the kind of relationship God wants with every person who calls Jesus "Lord."

Target #2: A Head Filled with Applied Wisdom from Scripture

The Bible says of itself in 2 Timothy 3:16-17, "All Scripture is God-breathed and is useful for teaching, rebuking, correcting and training in righteousness, so that the man [or woman] of God may be thoroughly equipped for every good work."

If our kids are to grow in their relationship with Him, they need to study it, learn it, and know how to apply its truths to life's challenges and choices.

They also need to realize that when God gives biblical guidelines for human conduct, it's not because He's out to make them miserable. Rather, He's like a parent who knows things His children don't—and issues instructions for their well-being.

Many of today's young Christians are woefully ignorant of God's Word. Recent surveys have shown that even students planning to attend Bible college or seminary lack basic biblical knowledge.

You can make sure this isn't true of your teen. But you need a plan, and you need to be working at it every day— studying the Bible together, memorizing it, and talking about how it applies in the nitty-gritty of life.

This isn't easy; it calls for commitment, determination, and prayer. But it's the only way. Fortunately, God will guide and strengthen you for the task.

Target #3: Skill in Filtering Life Through a Christian Worldview

Our ready-to-graduate teenagers need to know how to "think Christianly," and to make a habit of doing so. As they make decisions about work, spending money, choosing friends, voting, and more, they should do so from a scriptural perspective.

For example, a Christian teen who's offered a marijuana cigarette at a party and told that "everyone else is doing it" ought to know what 1 Corinthians 6:19-20 says: "Do you not know that your body is a temple of the Holy Spirit, who is in you, whom you have received from God? You are not your own; you were bought at a price. Therefore honor God with your body."

Looking at the situation through that filter, the teen will understand that more is at stake in his decision than just "Will I get caught?" or "Isn't it okay to give it a try this once?" Having this perspective doesn't guarantee that he'll make the right choice, but it may make him more likely to say a quick prayer asking for God's help to resist the temptation.

The mind-set we want to see in our children is summed up in the question, "What would Jesus do?" Whether or not they wear WWJD bracelets, that's the way we want them to look at the world.

Target #4: An Ability to Articulate and Defend the Bible

Our soon-to-be-on-their-own teens need to be able and willing to articulate and defend biblical standards to others. The Bible speaks to this aspect of faith when it says, "Always be prepared to give an answer to everyone who asks you to give the reason for the hope that you have. But do this with gentleness and respect" (1 Peter 3:15).

One 17-year-old named Melissa found out how difficult that can be. When she and her mom went to a taping of Oprah Winfrey's popular TV talk show in Chicago, she found herself defending biblical values. A producer had described Oprah as a Christian and explained that Oprah would be voicing support for her guest, comedienne Ellen DeGeneres, who would soon be "coming out" on her sitcom as a gay person. The producer asked whether anyone had a problem with that.

Melissa, aware that the Bible says God loves everyone but condemns homosexual conduct, felt compelled to speak up. "I said that I thought that it would be wrong for Oprah to go on the show and support Ellen in her homosexual lifestyle if she [Oprah] professes to be a Christian and upholds those values and believes in Jesus Christ, and that would just be a double standard, and she couldn't do it."

Other audience members either stayed silent or disagreed with Melissa. Still, the girl stated her position again for the TV cameras when invited to do so. As if that weren't tough enough, she also "got a lot of flak for it" when she went back to school.

Melissa had developed this aspect of her faith well.

Knowing the truth of Scripture and being willing to defend it publicly, she was able to do so gently and respectfully.

Target #5: Wanting to Make Christ Known Through Life, Work, Service, and Witness

A teen who has a personal and vibrant relationship with Jesus Christ will want to share the joy and hope of that relationship with others. Sometimes that will be done with words, but most often it will be done through example.

When a teen treats everyone—even the new kids at school and those whom others consider "weird"—with politeness and respect, people notice. When a teen works hard, does more than is expected, and volunteers to help the homeless or build a church as part of a missions trip, people wonder why. And when that teen publicly thanks God for the good things in his life, people listen.

A Faith Ready to Leave Home

As you look ahead to that high school graduation, you want your teen to have a faith in Jesus Christ that's personal, vibrant, biblically guided, strong enough to stand up for the truth with gentleness and respect, and put into action before a watching world.

It's a goal worthy of your best efforts. And, like most goals worth reaching, it will require them. But you're not alone in this quest. God is on your side.

steps to take

1. On each of the following targets, make a mark to show how close your teen is to a "bull's-eye":

A Personal, Vibrant Relationship with Jesus Christ

A Head Filled with Applied Wisdom from Scripture

Skill in Filtering Life Through a Christian Worldview

An Ability to Articulate and Defend the Bible

Wanting to Make Christ Known Through Life, Work, Service, and Witness

2. Which of the following is true for your teen?
   a. You know when he began a personal relationship with Christ
   b. You believe he has such a relationship because of the way he acts
   c. You aren't sure whether he has such a relationship
   d. You doubt he has such a relationship

   Based on your answer, which of these is most urgent?
   a. Asking your teen whether he has a personal relationship with Christ
   b. Asking whether he would like to begin such a relationship

c. Asking how that relationship has grown since it
   began
d. Building a level of honesty that enables you to ask
   questions like these

3. Which of the following do you think your teen can
   quote? Indicate the percentage of accuracy you believe
   she would achieve for each passage.

THE LORD'S PRAYER
100%   75%   50%   25%   0%

THE TEN COMMANDMENTS
100%   75%   50%   25%   0%

THE FRUIT OF THE SPIRIT (Galatians 5:22-23)
100%   75%   50%   25%   0%

PSALM 23
100%   75%   50%   25%   0%

THE BEATITUDES (Matthew 5:3-12)
100%   75%   50%   25%   0%

JOHN 3:16
100%   75%   50%   25%   0%

Try testing your teen this week to see how correct your
answers were.

Now circle the percentages that indicate how well you
think your teen *understands* the Bible passages.

Finally, circle the percentages that show how well you
think your teen has *applied* the principles of each passage to her life.

Based on your answers, do you need to work most with your teen on memorizing, understanding, or obeying the Bible?

4. In which two of the following areas do you think your teen is *least* likely to have a "Christian worldview"?
    a. Entertainment choices
    b. Voting
    c. Driving habits
    d. Sexual behavior
    e. Church attendance
    f. Career plans
    g. Work ethic

    Based on your answers, which of these areas do you need to work on most?

5. In which of the following ways are you willing to prepare your teen during the next month to defend his faith?
    a. Show him a video on intelligent design, like *Unlocking the Mystery of Life* (available from Focus on the Family)
    b. Give him a book about absolute truth, like *My Truth, Your Truth, Whose Truth?* (also available from Focus on the Family)
    c. As a family activity, stage a mock debate on Christianity
    d. Together on the Internet, look up examples of archaeological finds that substantiate the accuracy of the Bible
    e. Other _____

6. Which of the following methods of making Christ
known would come most naturally to your teen?
a. Talking to a friend
b. Speaking to a group
c. Working on a service project
d. Doing an everyday "good deed"
e. Other _____

How could you help your teen have the confidence to
do that?
a. Pray for him
b. Pray with him
c. Give him a pep talk
d. Show him how to do it
e. Join him in doing it
f. Other _____

4

Helping Your Teen to Own His Faith

Marilyn was five when she prayed the "sinner's prayer" at church. Later she couldn't remember why she decided to do it; all she knew was that her mother hugged her afterward and said it was a "great moment" in Marilyn's life.

Not long after that, Marilyn's parents divorced. Marilyn was raised under the watchful eyes of her mother and maternal grandparents, who forbade her to view or listen to anything other than Christian TV and radio. She attended the small Christian school sponsored by her church. She went to church camp in the summers, where she felt pressured to do the "right" things in order to prove she was a true believer.

Marilyn hated her life. She hated it when her mother called her a "teenager for Christ."

When the time came to go to college, it was Marilyn's chance to escape. She chose a school that didn't teach the doctrines of her childhood. She stopped going to church. Her professors encouraged her to think for herself. At last she had found the freedom she'd craved.

Before long, Marilyn's rejection of Christianity was complete. For a while, she felt twinges of guilt and fear that she might go to hell. But eventually those feelings went away, too.

Today Marilyn counts herself among those who have "walked away" from "fundamentalism." She says she will spend the rest of her life working toward being herself, something she was denied during her growing-up years.[1]

Marilyn's "faith" clearly was not her own. The "mentors" in her life pressed her to act the way they thought a believer should, but her conformity was strictly external.

You don't want Marilyn's story to be the story of your family. You want your adolescent's faith to be real and lifelong.

Discipleship begins with a personal choice to follow Jesus. As Marilyn's story shows, you can't make that choice for your teen. But you can help him understand the importance of having a vital, growing relationship with God—instead of simply trying to get your teen to "act like a Christian."

survey

1. **The story of Marilyn makes you want to**
   a. Throw a party
   b. Throw up your hands in despair
   c. Throw up
   d. Other _____

2. **Which of the following best describes your teen's convictions about absolute truth?**
   a. "God says it; I believe it; that settles it."
   b. "What's true for you may not be true for me."
   c. "It's not a lie if you cross your fingers, is it?"
   d. Other _____

3. **You can't give your faith to your teen, but you can**
   a. Encourage him to develop his own
   b. Loan it to him for up to 30 days at a time
   c. Tape it to his back like a "Kick Me" sign
   d. Other _____

4. **Your parents encouraged you to "own your faith" by**
   a. Supporting you when you had doubts
   b. Preparing you to answer skeptics
   c. Locking you in the closet until you agreed with them
   d. Other _____

5. **You want your teen to own her faith because**
   a. God looks on the heart
   b. You'd be embarrassed if she became an atheist
   c. It's cheaper than renting
   d. Other _____

scripture

1. Look at Acts 16:30-31. Has your teen taken this step? How do you know?

   If your answer to the previous question is yes, what are two other steps of faith you'd like to see your teen take before leaving home?

2. Read Matthew 13:3-9, 18-23. According to this parable, what are three reasons why a teen who seemed to start a relationship with God as a young child might no longer appear to have such a relationship?

What's one thing a parent can do to nurture the spiritual "seed" that's been planted in a young person's life?

3. Read James 2:14-19. What are three actions your teen has taken in the last year that indicate his or her faith is real?

If you can't answer the previous question, how do you feel about that?

4. Consider Proverbs 22:6. Many commentators believe this verse is not a promise, but a statement of a principle that's generally true. Do you agree? Why or why not?

If a child's spiritual training doesn't include the process of turning beliefs into personal convictions, what may happen when the child is "old"?

strategies

Is your teen a Christian?

Let's define our terms. For purposes of this book, let's say a Christian is one who's decided to receive God's gift of eternal life by placing his or her trust in Jesus Christ as Savior, and who wants to follow Him.

How can you tell whether your teen has made it to that point?

There are no formulas for assessing the spiritual state of another person, even when that person is your child. But here are some suggestions for getting a more accurate "read" on the teen who claims to be a Christian:

- *Look for fruit.* "I am the true vine, and my Father is the gardener," Jesus said. "He cuts off every branch in me that bears no fruit, while every branch that does bear fruit he prunes so that it will be even more fruitful" (John 15:1-2). While we are not called to "inspect" the fruit of others instead of our own, it should raise questions in our minds if a teenager displays *no* love for others, *no* willingness to obey God, and *no* interest in becoming more like Jesus (see 1 John 2:3-11).

- *Ask for an update.* Some young children make "decisions for Christ" that consist mainly of repeating a prayer or walking down an aisle; these incidents may be forgotten by the time adolescence arrives. Ask your teen to tell you what Jesus means to her *now*.

- *Check with peers.* Some teens lead Jekyll-and-Hyde lives, toeing the line at home and church but dumping Christian standards at school and with friends. While "spying" on your teen might be unwise, getting to know his friends and teachers probably will yield hints of a double life if one exists. If it does, ask your teen to tell you which self is the "real" one.

If your teen *has* made a decision for Christ and has a desire—even a small one—to follow Him, you have the foundation for discipleship. If not, you can encourage your teen to take that step.

How? Here are some ideas:

- *Make sure your teen understands the basics.* If your teen knows little or nothing about God, Jesus, or the Bible, this would be a good time to fill in those gaps.

Encourage her to read the Gospel of John and discuss it with you.

- *Ask for a decision, but don't press.* When your teen appears to understand the basics of what Jesus has done for him, simply ask something like, "Do you want to pray now to ask God to forgive you and to let you start a relationship with Him?" Using the word *now* makes it easier for your teen to pray on his own, or for you to ask again later if necessary.

- *Enlist the help of a youth leader.* If your teen isn't ready to make a commitment, she may be open to further exploration in a "neutral" setting away from your direct influence. Explain the situation to a leader in your church's youth ministry, and ask whether he or she can help provide opportunities for your teen to encounter the claims of Christ at a retreat, concert, camp, or youth group Bible study.

- *Encourage friendships with Christian teens.* The kids your teen spends time with will fuel in him either a desire to get closer to God or a desire to move further from Him. So know who his friends are, and encourage him to hang around with people who will bolster his spiritual appetite.

- *Pray.* The most important thing you can do to help your teen begin a relationship with God is to ask for His aid. And try to relax, leaving your teen's response with the God who has given your child the freedom to decide.

Turning Beliefs into Convictions

Once your teen chooses to accept Christ as Savior, he faces a multitude of other forks in the road. If you tell him that premarital sex is off-limits, for example, your teen can choose to ignore that belief, adopt it in theory but not in practice, or internalize it as a personal conviction.

In *Bound by Honor* (Tyndale/Focus on the Family,

1998), Gary and Greg Smalley tackle the issue of turning beliefs into convictions.

As the Smalleys point out, we can't *pass down* our convictions. That's because convictions must grow from the inside out. It happens when our teens struggle through their own questions, doubts, and trials.

We can help our kids with that struggle. The Smalleys suggest seven ways to help teens turn their beliefs into convictions:

1. *Remember that the relationship always comes first.* The two biggest factors in building a healthy relationship, say the Smalleys, are honoring your teen regularly and helping to keep her anger level low. Marilyn, who walked away from Christianity after years of being pressured to "act like a Christian," seethed her way through adolescence; instead of recognizing and addressing her anger, the adults in her life simply gave her more reasons to be angry.

2. *Sharpen your own convictions so you can be an effective model.* Children adopt our values during their early years—and question those values upon reaching adolescence. If our walk doesn't match our talk, we give our teens all the more reason to reject those values.

3. *Once you're modeling, provide formal instruction.* The focus of "formal" instruction is to help kids develop beliefs, which can deepen into convictions.

Formal doesn't have to mean stiff. Here it means being intentional and verbal, spending time with your teen and watching for "teachable moments" that provide opportunities for you to have a natural conversation about spiritual things.

4. *After instructing, allow teens to find their own answers.* Let teens explore conviction-building questions like the following—within boundaries determined by their demonstrated maturity, and with resources provided by you if needed:

- What do I really believe about the Bible?
- How much money should I spend on myself?
- What's my position on attending R-rated movies?
- What should I do if my friends are negatively influencing me?

5. *Provide encouragement during times of belief questioning.* We can do that by telling our teens we're proud that they're wrestling honestly with their questions. Rather than panicking and becoming defensive or preachy, we can empathize with the confusion and frustration they feel.

6. *Monitor teens during the belief-questioning process.* If 14-year-old Maya's doubts about the Bible lead her to skip classes at her Christian school, should you simply applaud her independence? If 16-year-old Alan's search spurs him to join a cult, should you just wave good-bye and say, "I hope you find what you're looking for"?

No. Kids need limits as well as freedoms. Family rules and limits can provide that kind of security.

The Smalleys suggest adding an article to the "family constitution" that reads, "We agree to give each teenager the opportunity to develop his or her own beliefs and convictions. We will allow the questioning of our family values. However, if we feel that harm will result from the questioning process, we will intervene and provide a boundary."

7. *Remember that conviction building is a process, not a quick fix.* Building convictions is a lifelong project. It can be painful, too. But as the Smalleys observed, "God has forever to mold their character. . . . The *beauty* of detours is that they're the very things that can produce a strong faith."

steps to take

1. Which of the following "fruit" have you seen in your teen's life during the last year?
   a. Increased interest in what the Bible has to say
   b. Concern for others

c. Sharing faith with a friend
d. Asking questions about spiritual things
e. Wanting to spend more time with Christians
f. Expressing enthusiasm about being a Christian
g. Other _____

What does your answer lead you to conclude about your teen's commitment to Christ?

2. Asking your teen to tell you what Jesus means to him or her now may elicit a revealing answer—or a vague one. To encourage specific responses, try reading the following list of words aloud. After each word, ask your teen whether that word describes something about his or her relationship to Jesus today—and why.

GUILT	HAPPINESS	RULES
STRENGTH	LOVE	BOREDOM
ADVENTURE	FORGIVENESS	HEAVEN
DOUBT	SACRIFICE	PUNISHMENT
HELP	RESCUE	OBEYING

3. Does your teen understand "the basics"? Check off all of the following concepts that you believe he or she grasps.

___ God exists.
___ Jesus is the Son of God.
___ All of us have sinned.
___ The penalty for sin is death.
___ Jesus, who never sinned, didn't deserve to die.
___ Jesus willing paid the penalty for everyone else.
___ All who accept Jesus' death as payment for their sins can be forgiven and have a relationship with God that lasts forever.

Now ask your teen to confirm whether he or she understands the concepts you've marked. Are there any surprises?

4. If you don't think your teen has trusted Christ as Savior, how would you feel about giving him or her the opportunity to do so this week?

If you were to ask your teen whether he or she would like to trust in Christ, in which of the following places would you feel most comfortable asking that question?

___ Kitchen

___ Living room

___ Family room

___ Bedroom

___ Car

___ Restaurant

___ Other _____

At which of the following times of day would you feel most comfortable asking that question?

___ First thing in the morning

___ Lunch

___ After school

___ Dinner

___ Evening (name time) _____

___ Bedtime

___ Other _____

On which day of the upcoming week would you want to ask that question?

___ Sunday
___ Monday
___ Tuesday
___ Wednesday
___ Thursday
___ Friday
___ Saturday

Are you willing to ask that question this week, in your preferred place at your preferred time? Why or why not?

5. If you think your teen hasn't placed his or her faith in Christ, praying for him or her is an excellent idea. In the space that follows, try writing a prayer that expresses what you'd like God to do in your teen's heart—and your willingness to be part of that process.

Lord,

6. When it comes to turning beliefs into convictions, which of the following questions are you willing to let your teen explore?

___ "Are there mistakes in the Bible?"

___ "Do I have to tithe?"

___ "Is it okay to watch movies that have swearing in them?"

___ "Is it possible that the Creation story in Genesis isn't meant to be taken literally?"

___ "Do animals have rights like people do?"

___ "Is abortion wrong?"

___ "Do all religions have truth in them?"

___ Other: _____

How will you let your teen know he or she is free to explore the questions you've marked?

7. How could you encourage your teen's constructive questioning in each of the following cases?

Your teen says: "If God loves everybody, why doesn't He let everybody go to heaven?"

You respond:

Your teen says: "How can Jesus be God and the Son of God?"

You respond:

Your teen says: "What's the point of going to church when it's so boring?"

You respond:

PART 2

Building a Great Relationship with Your Teen

5

The Ties
That Bond

Janna, age 17, had been dating Tom for nearly two years. Like many teen couples, they spent most of their waking hours together. They liked laughing, listening to music, and exploring side roads off the interstate. Everything inside Janna and everything Tom told her indicated they'd probably spend the rest of their lives together.

But then he broke up with her.

In her room, Janna sobbed until her chest hurt and her throat was raw. She curled up into a ball.

How could she get through this? Having recently moved far away from her friends, she felt so alone. She supposed she could talk to her parents, but everybody knew how adults felt about teen romances. They were "puppy love," infatuation, foolishness. Janna knew, though, that this was real enough to break her heart.

Finally she pulled herself together and went downstairs, trying hard to pretend everything was okay. Her mother, knitting on the sofa, called her over and patted the cushion next to her. Janna sat, looking at her hands folded in her lap.

"It must be very hard," her mother said softly. "I know how much you loved him."

Janna couldn't believe her ears. Her mother understood! She hadn't told Janna she was immature or that she wasn't capable of true love.

Because of that conversation, Janna was able to move forward through her grief. She also began to feel closer to her mother and to share more with her.

Janna's mom had made a crucial choice that day. She'd chosen to build a bridge to her daughter rather than deliver a condescending speech. As a result, Janna was more willing to accept her mom's guidance in matters of the spirit as well as of the heart.

As the parent of a teenager, you can make that choice as well. You can cultivate a relationship—even a friendship—with your teen that will last into adulthood. If you want to be a spiritual mentor to your young person, that relationship isn't a luxury. It literally can spell the difference between success and failure.

survey

1. The idea that teenagers are hard to get along with is
   a. A myth
   b. Sad but true
   c. Like saying sumo wrestlers are a bit pudgy
   d. Other _____

2. **The hardest part of living with teenagers is**
   a. Shepherding them through their daily emotional struggles
   b. Helping them to form their own identities
   c. Not being able to encase them in concrete and throw them in the river
   d. Other _____

3. **How do you prefer to express affection to your teen?**
   a. Through words
   b. Through touch
   c. From a distance of at least 12 miles
   d. Other _____

4. **If you try to impose rules without having a good relationship with your teen, you'll get**
   a. Rich
   b. Rebellion
   c. On one of those awful daytime TV talk shows
   d. Other _____

5. **Your teen knows you love her because**
   a. You say it every day
   b. You demonstrate it every day
   c. Your people faxed her people a document to that effect
   d. Other _____

scripture

1. Consider Exodus 20:1-6. In this passage, how does God remind the Israelites of His relationship with them before "laying down the law"?

   What kind of relationship with your teen would you like to establish before "laying down the rules"?

2. For each of the following verses, jot down the words and phrases that are easiest for you to practice in your relationship with your teen. Then write the ones that are hardest.

Verse: Romans 12:10
Easiest:
Hardest:

Verse: Romans 12:16
Easiest:
Hardest:

Verse: Romans 13:8
Easiest:
Hardest:

Verse: Romans 14:13
Easiest:
Hardest:

Verse: Romans 15:7
Easiest:
Hardest:

Verse: Galatians 5:13
Easiest:
Hardest:

Verse: Ephesians 4:2
Easiest:
Hardest:

Verse: Ephesians 4:32
Easiest:
Hardest:

Verse: Ephesians 5:21
Easiest:
Hardest:

Verse: Colossians 3:13
Easiest:
Hardest:

3. Read Ephesians 6:4. When's the last time you felt
   exasperated by someone? How did it affect your
   relationship?

How can you tell from this verse that spiritual mentoring should not, in itself, exasperate your teen?

If spiritual training seems to be a negative experience
for your teen, what might be the cause?

strategies

Without a strong, healthy relationship, spiritual mentoring
is merely a nice idea.

That's because rules without relationship lead to rebellion. Rex, a father, found that out one evening when he
turned down a request from his son Neil. Frustrated, the
boy lashed out: "You only care about Mom, work, God,
and Jesus!"

Rex resolved immediately to work on his relationship
with Neil. He didn't want to lose his influence with his
son—and knew that might happen if Neil saw himself as
being at the bottom of Dad's priority list.

When your teen knows you love him, he'll be more
willing to accept the idea that the rules and values you
want to pass along are in his best interest.

Family Ties

Being a spiritual mentor to your teen doesn't require a *perfect* relationship. But it must be genuine, caring, and reciprocating. That kind of bond doesn't come with the birth certificate. It requires efforts like the following.

Relationship Builder #1: Empathy

There's a step you can take right now, this minute, to start building a bridge to your adolescent.

You can remember what it was like to be a teenager yourself.

That may be a scary proposition, especially if your teen years were ones you'd rather forget. But it helps us to empathize with our kids. It tells us when to back off and when to step in—when to be strong, when to share, when to speak hard truths, and when to listen.

Relationship Builder #2: Respect

Some parents fall into the trap of rolling their eyes when talking about their child. They tell other adults, even in the teen's hearing, how difficult their son is to live with or how foolish their daughter's latest tears were.

When we treat anyone with such dishonor, what should we expect? The disrespected person will respond in kind—or become so disheartened that he'll never fulfill his potential.

Relationship Builder #3: Honesty

To forge and maintain an authentic bond with your teen, you'll need to tell the truth.

This doesn't mean you must divulge every secret in your life. But it does mean (1) telling no lies and (2) getting to the root of what your teen really wants to know—which probably has more to do with her options than with your past.

Usually honesty is a much simpler matter. It may even

boil down to saying those three little words many of us find hardest to choke out: "I don't know."

Relationship Builder #4: Listening

Teens are notorious for not talking. Yet many say they don't talk to their parents because their parents don't really listen. Here are some ways to be "all ears":

1. *Take time to listen.* If your teen hears time and again, "I'm busy—can we talk later?" he will eventually stop talking to you.

2. *Just listen, period.* Listening isn't judging or jumping in to "fix" things. There will be time to offer your thoughts when the task of listening has been completed.

3. *Listen even when it's tough.* Listening may mean hearing things you don't want to hear. If you want to strengthen your relationship, listen anyway.

4. *Consider carefully what you hear.* Tim, a high-school senior, wants to talk to his father about the 11:00 curfew he's had since his freshman year. Tim's dad feels himself tensing but resists the urge to panic. As it turns out, Tim has some good ideas.

Dad breathes a sigh of relief, glad that he didn't end the discussion too soon. He promises to think seriously about his son's suggestions and to talk again tomorrow. Tim feels respected, valued—listened to.

Relationship Builder #5: Fun

"I want my kids to like me," says Joe White. "I want them not to drink and hang out because I'm more fun than 'Miller time.'"

Good times with your teen will give you strength to face hard times the relationship is bound to bring. Fun times together remind your teen that you're not just a disciplinarian—and that you're interested in many aspects of his life, not just his behavior.

Relationship Builder #6: Affection

If your teen doesn't get affection at home, he or she will go elsewhere for it.

Sadly, some parents feel that when a child becomes a teenager, the time for affectionate words and touch is past. Dads feel especially awkward when their girls blossom into young women, fearing it would be inappropriate to hug them. But a father can always give his teen daughter "Daddy hugs"—brief, one-arm-around-the-shoulder squeezes.

Here are more suggestions:

1. *Touch caringly and carefully.* Some families make it a rule that one hug or kiss a day must be exchanged. When you speak with your teen, try touching her on the arm or shoulder. Moms can offer to braid a daughter's hair; Dads can wrestle with a son.

2. *Express affection in words, too.* One father never ends a phone chat with a family member without an enthusiastic "I love you!"—even when he's at the office.

3. *Don't push it.* If your teen would be embarrassed by displays of affection in front of his friends, wait for a better time. But don't be fooled into thinking that a standoffish teen needs no affection at all.

Relationship Builder #7: Vulnerability

Your teen needs to see the reality of God in your life—and that your relationship with Him has its ups and downs. It's okay, even beneficial, for your young person to know that you have questions, and for the two of you to go to the Bible together for answers.

All-too-human believers can make great parents—and spiritual mentors.

Relationship Builder #8: Erasing Bitterness Daily

Garbage stinks. That's why we keep taking it out.

The "garbage" of unresolved anger in your relationship with your teen must be disposed of as soon as possible. Otherwise, it can distance you from your teen.

If you think your teen is angry with you, but you don't know why, ask him. Then listen carefully and respond gently, quietly, and slowly. If you were wrong, admit it.

If your teen doesn't want to open up, give her time and space to work through her emotions alone while allowing her opportunities to speak with you. An exchange of letters at this point might be helpful.

Relationship Busters

Every job has its list of don'ts. Forging a bond with your teen is no exception.

1. *Never attack your teen verbally or physically.* Instead of condemnation, she needs guidance to move from a bad choice to a better one. Don't discipline your teen in front of his peers. If an issue needs to be dealt with immediately, take him to another room and speak quietly there.

2. *Don't stop being a parent.* If you've established a boundary and your teen deliberately crosses it, the boundary must be enforced. Rules without love lead to rebellion, but so does love without rules.

3. *Don't treat your teen as a "typical adolescent."* Do you relate to your teen as an individual? Do you suspect him of lying because "all" kids lie? We can't build relationships with "types," only with people.

4. *Don't resist outside help.* If your relationship continues to struggle, don't be afraid to seek assistance from your pastor or a counselor. Resolve to work on yourself and your relationship with your teen, whatever it takes.

steps to take

1. Think about *your* favorite relationships. Make a check mark next to the following phrases that describe the kind of person you like to spend time with. Then make

two check marks next to phrases that describe the kind
of parent you think your teen would like to spend time
with.

___ Someone who loves you
___ Someone who sees your strengths and compli-
      ments you on them
___ Someone who listens to you and respects your
      opinions even if he doesn't agree with you
___ Someone who's affectionate verbally and physically
___ Someone who respects your boundaries
___ Someone who's fun to be with
___ Someone who honestly shares himself and his
      stories
___ Someone who's interested in developing a genuine
      relationship with you
___ Someone who wouldn't ridicule you
___ Someone who forgives you
___ Someone who embraces all of who you are—good
      and bad, struggles and successes

Which of the double-checked phrases describe you?

Which ones indicate areas you need to work on?

2. Need help to remember what it was like to be a
   teenager, in order to empathize? Try writing your
   answers to these questions:

   When you were your teen's age, who did you wish you
   were?

Whom did you hope to become?

What were your deepest hurts? How did they feel?

What did you usually do when faced with a crisis?

How did you feel when your friends were involved in something that you knew wasn't right? What did you do?

If you could travel back in time and be a friend to your teenage self, what advice would you offer? What comfort? How might that advice and comfort be received?

3. The following is a real letter from a teen to an adult who treated him more respectfully than other grown-ups usually did:

"You treated me as I would assume you treat most of your children's friends: as adults. That's so hard for us to find. You understand that kids are smart enough to start making their own decisions about things and come to their own conclusions. Many adults look at them as know-it-all brats with little experience and patronize at best."

Would your teen write a similar note about you? Why or why not?

4. Gail, a single mom, has made it a rule that she won't open her daughter's mail, notes, or journals. After all, Gail wouldn't want anyone digging through her own purse, briefcase, desk, or clothing drawers. She wouldn't want anyone eavesdropping on her phone conversations or reading her private writings, either. (Gail allows, however, that if her daughter seemed to be involved in dangerous behavior, she probably would break the rule for the girl's protection.)

How does Gail's privacy policy compare to yours?

How does your privacy policy affect your relationship with your teen?

5. Which three of the following parent-teen activities might have the most positive effect on your relationship?

___ Air hockey
___ Baking cookies
___ Training a dog or horse together
___ Going to a concert (your favorite music)
___ Going to a concert (his or her favorite music)
___ Crafts
___ Going to an English-style tea

___ Go-kart racing
___ Rock climbing
___ Visiting a museum
___ Table tennis
___ One-on-one shopping
___ Skating
___ Skiing
___ Stargazing
___ Taking a group of his or her friends out for pizza
 or ice cream
___ Laser tag
___ Paintball
___ Seeing a play at the high school
___ Miniature golf
___ Looking at used cars

Now pick one of the activities you checked and plan to enjoy it with your teen this week.

6. Which of these physical expressions of affection do you think your teen would appreciate from you? Which do you feel comfortable giving? Make a check mark next to those that qualify in both categories.
___ Pat on the back
___ Arm around the shoulders
___ High five
___ Handshake
___ Quick stroke of the hair
___ Pat on the knee (especially while driving, sitting in church, or watching television together)
___ Shoulder massage
___ Back scratch
___ Kiss on the cheek or forehead

7. In the space below, draw a map of your spiritual journey through adolescence. You may want to include some mountaintop experiences, valleys of despair, frustrating detours, and rivers of refreshment. Share your map with your teen and ask him to make one for you that describes his own spiritual trek so far.

6

Learning to Be a Great Communicator

startup

"Patrick, how was youth group tonight?"

"Okay, I guess."

"What did you do?"

"Nothing."

"What was it about?"

"Stuff."

"Did you get anything out of it?"

"No."

"Why not?"

Shrug.

"Your sister always got something out of the small groups."

Grunt.

"Don't you?"

"Sometimes."

"What's something you've gotten out of the small groups?"

"It's personal."

"If you won't tell me, maybe I should ask your small-group leader."

Hard glare.

"Don't give me that look or you'll be grounded."

"Fine."

Ah, the joys of spiritual mentoring.

Communicating is crucial to giving spiritual guidance, but trying to communicate with teenagers can be a good way to jump-start a headache. Many parents are baffled by one-word responses from a son or daughter who routinely spends three hours a day on the phone with friends.

To make matters worse, real communication involves far more than just talking *at* someone. It's even more than listening to someone convey information.

Communication is part of the relationship-building process. Perhaps that's why the *American Heritage Collegiate Dictionary* defines communication this way: "To be connected, one with another."

survey

1. **The best way to start a conversation with your teen is by asking,**
   a. "Is there anything you'd like to talk about?"
   b. "Why is your hair on fire?"
   c. "How much money may I give you today?"
   d. Other _____

2. **You can tell your teen is listening to you when he**
   a. Leans forward slightly and looks you in the eye
   b. Frowns thoughtfully and scratches his chin
   c. Stares at you as if you're drooling
   d. Other _____

3. **You and your teen communicate best when**
   a. You're sitting at the kitchen table
   b. You're eating in a restaurant
   c. You've both taken too much cold medication
   d. Other _____

4. **It's hardest for you and your teen to talk about**
   a. Politics, religion, and sex
   b. Politics, religion, sex, music, school, friends, clothes, and quantum physics
   c. Everything except passing the ketchup
   d. Other _____

5. **If you ask your teen how his day went, he usually**
   a. Mumbles something incoherent and goes to his room
   b. Mutters something indecipherable and goes to the refrigerator
   c. Engages you in polite, heartfelt conversation until you awaken from your dream
   d. Other _____

scripture

1. Check out Proverbs 15:1. Have you ever found this verse to be true as you've communicated with your teenager? If so, what happened?

2. Read James 1:19-20. Let's say your teen comes home three hours after curfew. You've been worried sick that he was in a car accident; now you want to break his guitar over his head. According to this passage, what should you do?

3. Read Ephesians 4:15. At which of the following times would it be hardest to tell your teen the truth: (a) when you don't approve of the guy she's been dating, (b) when you know his efforts to get into an Ivy League college will fail, or (c) when you can't afford to pay for car insurance so she can start driving? Why?

    At which of the following times would it be hardest to speak the truth in a *loving* way: (a) when your teen has been fired from his summer job for repeatedly showing up late, (b) when your teen has embarrassed you by swearing in front of the youth pastor, or (c) when your teen has slammed her door in your face because you told her to clean her room? Why?

4. Look at Proverbs 16:24. Other than "I love you" and "Here's some money," what three words from you might sound sweetest to your teen? When's the last time you said those words?

5. Consider Proverbs 12:25. At which of the following times of day is your teen most likely to be anxious and need a kind word: (a) right before school, (b) right after school, or (c) at bedtime? Why?

6. Read Proverbs 25:11. Which part of "aptly speaking" with your teen is hardest for you: (a) using the right tone of voice, (b) picking the right time to say things, (c) knowing what to say, or (d) something else?

strategies

There's no magic pill for communicating with adolescents. Every teen is unique; what might work for one won't work for another. Trying the following suggestions won't guarantee that a quiet, withdrawn teen will suddenly become talkative and eager to share. But they're a good place to begin.

How to Start a Conversation with Your Teen
When you want to get your teen talking, ask questions.

Starting a conversation with an adolescent is often like trying to get bread to rise in the cold. It's not going to happen unless you add a bit of yeast and warmth—and wait patiently. Ask your teen some well-thought-out questions (yeast), position yourself to listen attentively (warmth), and often you'll get a response.

If your teen seems to have something on his mind, ask, "Do you want to talk about it?" This leaves the door open for him to decide whether or not to open up. A "no" needs to be respected. You can ask the question again later.

Here are some conversation starters worth trying:

"What was the best thing that happened to you today?"

"What's going well?"

"What's not going well?"

"What's coming up in your schedule?"

"Is there anything you need my help with?"

When, Where, and How to Talk

One key to successful communication with your teen is knowing the best times, places, and ways in which to talk with him. Is your child more relaxed and open in the morning or evening? That may be the time to talk about feelings.

When does she tend to be most alert? That may be the time to discuss facts, worldviews, and rules.

Is your teen rushed during certain times of the day or week? Avoid starting complex conversations at those moments.

Taking your teen's mood into account is also critical in deciding whether to address a topic now or later. If he's in a funk, it may be best to postpone conversation. If your teen tends to have month-long funks, however, you may need to warn him in advance that a conversation on a particular topic is pending. Asking him to set the time for the chat within the next five days might help him to feel more prepared and cooperative.

As for the best place to talk, think about the spots in which you feel most comfortable chatting. Different kinds of discussions should happen in different places. Sitting on your teen's bed may be the best spot for sharing emotions or bringing up prayer requests. The living room might feel too open for a private, heartfelt conversation— but could be the right place to review what was discussed at the youth retreat. Restaurants are also a popular place to talk, especially if your past conversations in such places have been casual and safe.

And how should you talk? Tone of voice can be a conversation booster or breaker. If you dare, record yourself talking and analyze the result. Or ask your spouse or a friend to review your typical manner of speech and its possible effects on your teen.

Body language is also important. Next time you're talking with your teen, try keeping the following in mind:

- Lean forward, making positive eye contact, and nod occasionally to show that you're eager to hear what your teen has to say.
- Watch your teen's body language. Does it match her words? If not, you may need to ask some gentle questions. Do his posture and gestures hint at apprehension? If so, you may need to allow more time for him to open up.

Communicating During Conflict

Sometimes communication is more than hard—it's practically hopeless.

When family therapist Carleton Kendrick speaks at parenting seminars, he tells the story of an adolescent girl who'd been sullen toward her parents for months. One day she was on her way out the door to go to the movies with her friends.

Mom said, "Have a good time!"

The daughter turned around and snapped, "How dare you tell me what to do!"

No matter how hard you work at it, there will be times when communicating with your teen is virtually impossible. When your teen is in surly mode, try the following ways to show your love:

- Instead of insisting on conversation, be available to talk without pressuring.
- Respond to hurtful words by saying something like, "When you act like this toward me, it hurts me. I was only trying to help."
- Try communicating via a notebook or e-mail, to defuse the tension of face-to-face conversation. Write

a message and let him read it at his leisure. List things you appreciate about your teen; encourage him to write about questions, fears, frustrations, anger, and joy. Write for understanding, not to fuel a war.

Arguing Fairly

Married couples find it important to learn how to argue fairly. Some parents, on the other hand, seem to feel they should win all arguments with their teens. The truth is that both parents and teens are fallible, and both may have points that need to be made when there's a disagreement.

To start with, make sure the argument is necessary in the first place. Then be sure you have the following four elements required for resolving conflicts fairly:

1. *A willingness to admit your own role in the conflict.* Parents have been known to point fingers without acknowledging their own contribution to the dispute.

2. *The desire to work things out.* If you want to find a win-win solution, it's likely that you eventually will. But if your goal is to control your teen as you did when he or she was a child, you'll find only increased conflict.

3. *A focus on the present and future.* Avoid bringing up the past; stick with the topic at hand. Aim for a more peaceful future.

4. *A commitment to listening.* Commit yourself to listening even when it's painful. Decide to distinguish between anger and disrespect in your teen's tone of voice; forbid the latter, but acknowledge the former.

Once you've assembled those four tools, you can interact constructively. In *Bound by Honor*, Greg and Gary Smalley recommend the following steps for doing so:

1. *Clearly define the issues.* Without getting lost on tangents, identify the problem and work on that.

2. *Let the other person speak without interrupting.* If it will help you to listen better, keep a piece of paper handy to jot points down so you don't forget them.

3. *Create solutions.* Listing pros and cons of each potential solution is often helpful.

4. *Agree on solutions.* Sometimes this means not following through on the solution either the teen or the parent originally felt was correct. You may come up with a third course that combines both your preferences.

5. *Write down the agreement, and have all parties concerned sign it.* This will avoid confusion later.

Don't Give Up!

Good communication leads to heart-connections that will never break. No loving parent—and no spiritual mentor—can do without those links.

Years from now, when your teen has grown and left home but still lives by the spiritual values you taught and stays in touch, you'll be glad you made the effort to keep those cables connected.

steps to take

1. One way to gauge how well you've been communicating with your teen is to see how well you know his or her world. Try answering the following questions.

   What are your teen's favorite stores? What would she buy there if she could?

   How easy would it be for your teen to get illegal drugs?

   How many of your teen's friends drink alcohol?

   What are your teen's three favorite songs? What are the lyrics?

How many murders does your teen think he's seen on movie and TV screens in the last year?

Has your adolescent viewed pornography on the Internet?

What video games are most popular right now, and what does your teen think of them?

Does your teen worry about what she would do if a "shooter" opened fire at school?

How much pressure does your young person feel to cheat on exams?

Does your teen know anyone who's been sexually abused?

Does your teen have more "virtual" friends in chat rooms than in the real world?

If your teen defended the idea of absolute truth in front of his friends, would they laugh?

To check your answers, put these questions to your teen this week. You may find it's a good way to start a conversation.

2. Author Lissa Johnson tells this story about communicating with her teenager:

My daughter had a best friend we'll call Laura. They'd been friends since early elementary school, but now Laura was going through a tough time. Her clothing and makeup were seductive, she sported purple marks on her neck, and she was involved in other destructive behaviors.

I knew my daughter was at her own rebellious point, not wanting to do what I asked. How could I tell her not to spend time with Laura anymore? If I laid down the law, I felt my daughter would only become defiant and see Laura secretly.

Instead of preparing a lecture, I decided to speak to my daughter *as though she were a friend I was concerned about.*

With that in mind, I talked with her about Laura's behaviors. I told her I could see her beginning to slip in her own convictions by hanging out with Laura. Did she really want that? Was it really helping Laura to continue to hang out with her? We talked about how to be Laura's friend from a distance for the time being—still loving her and not snubbing her.

I told my daughter to think about it and get back to me. A day or two later, she reported her conclusion: that Laura was a bad influence on her, and she was going to distance herself from Laura for a while.

In time, Laura came back around—and the two were close friends again. Meanwhile, I'd discovered a way to give counsel and stay close to my daughter, too.

What do you think of the idea of talking to your teen as though he were a friend?

How does the way you communicate with your teen differ from the way you'd address a friend?

Choose a day this week when you'll address your teen as you would a friend. Write the day here.

Then, after you've tried it, write a short report about what happened.

3. Read the following to your teen.

Here are eight things kids generally want from a conversation with a parent:
1. Your attention
2. To be listened to, from beginning to end, without interruption
3. For you to care about what they say
4. For their secrets to be kept
5. To express their feelings
6. To be asked their opinion
7. To hear honestly about your own failures
8. To hear an understanding of his or her world

Here are eight things no teenager wants:
1. To be "talked down to"
2. To be pushed away
3. For you to get in his or her face
4. To be blasted with Bible verses or a sermon
5. To be judged or ridiculed for what he or she says
6. Unsolicited advice
7. For you to freak out
8. To hear adult clichés

Then ask your teen whether he agrees with these lists. Is there anything he'd add to either one? Is there anything on the first list he isn't getting from conversations with you? Is there anything on the second list he's getting and doesn't want?

7

Giving Grace

Joe White sat peering at the screen, watching videotapes of his son Brady playing high-school basketball. Joe planned to give Brady the edited result—a "highlights of basketball" video—as a graduation present.

As Joe viewed the scenes, however, he noticed something: This had been a tough year in basketball for Brady.

Still, that didn't prevent Joe from coming up with a good-looking tape. He simply fast-forwarded through the times when Brady had tossed the ball away or missed a shot, and he kept the successful three-pointers, passes, and drives. The final product looked like an NBA all-star highlight film!

In the middle of this editing session, it was as if the Lord spoke quietly to Joe: "As I edit the videotape of your life, watching you struggle from day to day, I know you're going to throw the ball away. I know you're going to make bad shots. But My highlight video of you is of all the good shots you made. It's all the things you did that were profitable or left fruit on the tree of life. When you get to heaven and we pull out the video, that's the tape I'm going to show you. And your assignment as a daddy is to be that kind of an editor for your children. When they make mistakes, deal with them and then edit those out, tossing them in the trash can forever."

Forgetting your teen's mistakes is one of the greatest gifts you can give him. You can choose to make "highlights" tapes or "bloopers" tapes.

Yes, there are times when we need to say something to our teens about their errors. There are times when disciplinary action is required. Once we've taken those steps, however, it's time to edit the day's tape and put the embarrassing footage in the trash can.

We need to be mirrors, reflecting back to our kids the unconditional love we get from God. Kids who experience that are motivated—excited about going to youth group, about serving, about Bible study, about leading godly lives. They're excited about grace.

survey

1. **A good definition of "grace" is**
   a. Unmerited favor
   b. Asking the blessing
   c. What you do when you're too tired to punish your kids
   d. Other _____

2. **God's grace to you has been most like**
   a. A refreshing rain
   b. A debt you can never repay
   c. A box of chocolates you don't want to share
   d. Other _____

3. **If your teen's life is like a videotape,**
   a. You hope it's on Extra Long Play
   b. You'd rather watch it with the sound off
   c. You still don't know how to program the VCR
   d. Other _____

4. **When you show grace, it enables your teen to**
   a. Resume spiritual growth with a clean slate
   b. Learn how to give grace to others
   c. Get away with murder
   d. Other _____

5. **The last time you showed grace to your teen**
   a. He showed you grace in return
   b. You regretted it for the rest of your life
   c. The Beatles were still together
   d. Other _____

scripture

1. Read Matthew 18:23-35. Who showed grace (undeserved favor) in this story, and who didn't?

   In the following space, try retelling the story with a twist. The first servant is the parent of a teenager; the master is God; and the fellow-servant is the teenager.

2. Look at Mark 14:66-68. On a scale of 1 to 10 (10 being highest), how serious an offense do you think it was for Peter to deny Jesus?

If a friend had done this to you, would you forgive him? Why or why not?

Read John 21:14-15. This took place after Peter's denial and Jesus' death. How did Jesus demonstrate grace here?

Why do you suppose Jesus gave Peter an assignment? Why not just say, "I forgive you," and put him on probation?

If this conversation hadn't taken place, what do you think the rest of Peter's life would have been like?

3. Look up Romans 5:8 and 1 John 4:19. How could you make the first move in showing grace to your teen—even though he or she might not deserve it?

strategies

Grace is the audacious but biblical idea that beginning a personal relationship with a holy God requires no work on our part—only accepting for ourselves the work of Jesus Christ. Even though our wrongdoing should result in lethal punishment, we're offered forgiveness and life—a second chance to go out there and get it right.

This outrageous gift is to be extended in our relationships. Because God's mercy has been great toward us, our mercy can be great toward our teens.

Spiritual Growth and Failure

In a relationship with God, there's plenty of failure. There will be times in every teen's life when, no matter how great the desire to do one thing, something else will be done instead.

Take, for example, the struggle many teens face concerning masturbation. Failure in an area like this can scuttle a teenager's efforts to maintain a close relationship with God. What can a spiritual mentor do to help a teen cope with such failure? Extend grace, as Dr. James Dobson advised:

> I would suggest that parents talk to their twelve- or thirteen-year-old boys, especially, in the same general way my mother and father discussed this subject with me. We were riding in the car, and my dad said, "Jim, when I was a boy, I worried so much about masturbation. It really became a scary thing for me because I thought God was condemning me for what I couldn't help. So I'm telling you now that I hope you don't feel the need to engage in this act when you reach the teen years, but if you do, you shouldn't be too concerned about it. I don't believe it has much to do with your relationship with God."
>
> What a kind thing my father did for me that night in the car. He was a very conservative minister who never compromised his standards of morality to the day of his death. He stood like a rock for biblical principles and commandments. Yet he cared enough about me to lift from my shoulders the burden of guilt that nearly destroyed some of my friends in the church. This kind of "reasonable" faith taught to me by my parents is one of the primary reasons I never felt it necessary to rebel against parental authority or defy God.[1]

This is not to say that masturbation should never be a cause for concern. But as with other struggles our teens experience, it is best approached with grace in mind. Grace makes it possible for spiritual growth to continue despite failure.

Modeling How to Handle Failure

When your teen sees you dealing with your own failures, can she tell that grace is part of the equation?

Bette is a mom who berates herself audibly and at great length when she makes a mistake. Her guilt is palpable when she confesses at family devotions, "I'm just terrible at remembering to pray during the day. I'm sure God isn't very happy with me."

Jerry, on the other hand, is a dad who tries to hide his mistakes. He fools no one, but believes his façade of perfection will inspire his teenage son to reach for "a high standard."

Though the approaches of Bette and Jerry are different, they share something in common: Their children, watching their examples, will learn little or nothing about grace. Even the apostle Paul, who did many things right, made mistakes. But he admitted that fact and kept moving ahead, growing: "Not that I have already obtained all this, or have already been made perfect, but I press on to take hold of that for which Christ Jesus took hold of me" (Philippians 3:12).

Be a Great Forgiver

God's relationship with us is characterized by forgiveness. So it should be in our relationships with our teens. Forgiveness cuts the chains of sin and guilt and releases us to find freedom and new direction.

In his role as director of Kanakuk Kamps, Joe White has seen many teens who desperately needed forgiveness. He tells the story of one in particular:

Rob was a very unusual camper. I'm not sure how he got to Kanakuk, since most of our kids are from very godly homes. Yet Rob came to camp saying he wanted to "kill the director."

When I met him, I discovered Rob was born to a 14-year-old mother and a 15-year-old father who were killed in an accident when he was eight years old. His rage and anger translated into numerous fights and encounters with the law. He was probably the angriest young man I've ever met. He'd been in a teen lockup facility for four years and involved in fights there. His hands were scarred from those fights.

As soon as he got off the bus, we asked to see his luggage to make sure—as we do with all kids—that there was nothing unsafe inside. He lashed out at me, wanting to take me out—as he had been doing with others for so many years.

Ironically, tattooed across Rob's back in two-inch letters was the word *forgiven*. Yet Rob knew nothing about forgiveness. His home environment was filled with rage.

Over the course of the next two weeks, I had the privilege of showing Rob unconditional love. Even though he tried to beat me up the first night of camp, I returned the anger with love and warmth and unconditional regard—which is my privilege as the "father" of these campers.

Two weeks went by, and one night I observed this boy—who had never really seen freedom as a teenager—watch and truly experience the sunset. As I walked by after the sun had set, Rob came to me with tears streaming down his face. He threw his arms around me, hugged me, and wept on my shoulder for five minutes. I quietly held him.

He looked at the scars on his hands and said, "I can't believe I've been this horrible to people my whole life—unnecessarily hitting people. Coach, I saw a beautiful painting in the sky tonight, and I knew that the painting had to have a painter."

I said, "Rob, you know what's better than that?"

"What?"

"To know that painter as a personal Friend."

Rob, who always had the last word, said, "You know what's better than that?"

I asked, "What?"

"To take that personal Friend into your heart and take Him home with you."

And so Rob gave his heart to Jesus.

That word *forgiven,* the word tattooed across his back, had become reality in his life for the first time. Rob found forgiveness. And he felt forgiven. The strength that forgiveness gave him enabled him to go back to his gang to pay off his $753 drug debt—and turn his back on the lifestyle and gang he'd been heavily involved in.

Forgiveness jump-starts new beginnings. The forgiven teen can find the strength to strive for secondary virginity, to turn away from violence, or to make a parent proud again.

When we forgive our teens, we show them grace. And we offer what God wants to give them for the rest of their lives—one chance after another to keep growing closer to Him despite their mistakes.

steps to take

1. Which of the following could help you feel God's grace toward you?

   a. Reading more about it in the Bible

   b. Watching a movie about Christ's sacrifice on the cross

c. Thinking about some of your sins He's forgiven
d. Listening to songs like "Amazing Grace" and "Wonderful Grace of Jesus"
e. Other _____

Which of those steps will you take this week?

2. In which of these areas has your teen seemed to let you down during the last year?
   a. Drinking or drug use
   b. Sexual activity
   c. Studying
   d. Spiritual growth
   e. Other _____

3. What would your teen have to do before you could forgive him or her for letting you down?
   a. Apologize
   b. Earn back my trust
   c. Change his or her behavior
   d. Suffer a penalty
   e. Other _____

4. How does your answer to the previous question compare with what you know of God's attitude toward forgiving you?

5. Reread the stories of Bette and Jerry in the "Modeling How to Handle Failure" section. Are you more like Bette or Jerry?

If you're more like Bette, what should you say to your teen next time you make a mistake?

If you're more like Jerry, what should you say to your teen next time you make a mistake?

6. If your teen asked for a "second chance," which of the following would it most likely be?
   a. To use the car after a traffic violation
   b. To go out again after breaking curfew
   c. To regain your trust after telling a lie
   d. To use the computer after going to forbidden Web sites
   e. Other _____

If you gave your teen that second chance, what do you think he or she would do with it?

If you're willing to grant that second chance, how will you announce it?

7. Which of these new beginnings would you most like to give your teen by showing him grace?
   a. Being able to approach God without feeling guilty
   b. Being able to approach you without feeling condemned
   c. Being able to dream big dreams

d. Being able to share his faith without feeling like a
   hypocrite
e. Other _____

How will you know when you've reached that goal?

Would anything about your relationship need to
change before that can happen?

What's one step you can take this week toward that
goal?

8

Becoming Your Teen's Biggest Fan

startup

It's near the end of the football game. The home team is behind by two points, thanks to a series of fumbles. It's third down and 16 to go. The home players' shoulders slump.

Suddenly a string of perky girls appears in front of the grandstand. The young ladies put their energy into motion, chanting, getting the crowd to shout with them:

Our stupid team
Does its best to make us scream!
Losers!
Losers!

No, wait. That's not how it happens.

Instead, the cheerleaders are there to encourage the team—no matter how far behind it is, no matter what mistakes it has made. Even if the game is lost, the cheerleaders will be back next week—cheering the team on as though the last defeat had never occurred.

Spiritual growth is a little like football. Your teen may gain yardage one week, only to lose it the next. There will be plenty of fumbles. Through it all, your adolescent needs someone to keep calling from the sidelines, "You can do it!"

You are that someone. As a parent, you've been elected head cheerleader.

That may not seem to come naturally, at least not at first. Most parents find it easy to be members of their babies' and toddlers' fan clubs, but many lose their enthusiasm by the time their children reach the teen years. Yet kids, especially those in today's world, never outgrow the need for regular shots of praise that send them into the day with hope.

survey

1. **When you were a teen, how often did your parents say something encouraging to you?**
   a. At least once a day
   b. Once a week, unless you hadn't taken a shower recently
   c. On your birthday, instead of giving you a present
   d. Other _____

2. **The difference between flattering your teen and praising him is**
   a. The degree of your sincerity
   b. Your motivation

    c. Not worth mentioning, since you don't plan to do
       either

    d. Other _____

3. **When is it hardest to encourage your teen?**
    a. When she's feeling guilty about a bad habit
    b. When she's feeling depressed about a broken dream
    c. When she's strangling you with one hand and picking your pocket with the other
    d. Other _____

4. **What was the last spiritual achievement for which you praised your teen?**
    a. Sharing his faith with a friend
    b. Memorizing a difficult Bible passage
    c. Not knocking over the flannelgraph when he was in the beginners' Sunday school class
    d. Other _____

5. **What kind of touch is most encouraging to your teen?**
    a. Putting an arm around his shoulder
    b. Kissing him on the top of his head
    c. Pressing a slice of Meat Lover's pizza into the palm of his hand
    d. Other _____

scripture

1. Read 1 Thessalonians 5:11. How is encouraging your teen like encouraging an adult acquaintance at church? How is it different?

In which of the following areas does your teen most need to be "built up": (a) concern about his or her appearance, (b) confidence in making friends, (c) belief that God loves him or her, (d) hope for his or her future, or (e) something else?

2. Look up Hebrews 3:13. On average, how many times per day do you say or write something encouraging to your teen? Are you satisfied with that? Do you think he or she is?

3. Check out 1 Thessalonians 5:14. When it comes to spiritual growth, does your teen tend to be idle, timid, or weak? According to this verse, does he or she most need warnings, encouragement, or help?

In which of these areas does your teen tend to be most timid: (a) sharing her faith, (b) dreaming big dreams, (c) asking God for things, (d) getting involved with others at church, or (e) standing up to peer pressure?

Based on your previous answer, what do you most need to encourage your teen to be or do?

4. Look at Romans 12:15. Does this verse mean that you should "cheer" only when your teen is celebrating, and avoid cheering when he's sad? Explain.

5. Read Proverbs 25:20. When might a parent's "cheer-leading" be annoying to a teen? How can you tell when to back off and let your teen be "heavyhearted" for a while?

strategies

Whether or not you shook any pom-poms in high school, you can excel as a cheerleader now. Here are six ways to get started:

Cheer #1: Don't Miss the Game

It's hard to cheer your teen on if you're absent when he takes the field. Are you around when your son competes in the speech tournament or runs the cross-country race? Are you there when your daughter sings in church or leaves for the youth group retreat?

To make things easier on yourself, regularly ask your teen for his schedule, and immediately put key events on your calendar.

When you face multiple events at the same time with more than one child, send Mom to one and Dad to the other. Next time, alternate. If you're a single parent, ask a close relative or friend to attend the other child's activity. Be sure to switch for the next event.

After the activity, take time to tell your teen how proud you are of him. If there's a tangible memento of the event (a program from a school play, a trophy, a photo, a certificate), display it on the refrigerator, mantel, or other prominent place in the house.

Cheer #2: Encourage Their Socks Off

Chances are that your teen has a lot of discouraging days. After getting her ego ripped apart or slowly eroded away, she needs to know she can come home and find encouragement.

Encouraging your teen can happen in a variety of ways:

- *Speak your encouragement.* This is especially effective when you praise your teen to someone else within your teen's hearing. Tell others what you like about your child—not just good grades or tennis skills, but also character traits like integrity and faithfulness.
- *Write your encouragement.* Tuck a note into a lunch sack or binder; sneak a greeting card into a backpack. The message can be as short as "I'm proud of you," "Have a good day—I'm praying for you," or "I love you like crazy." When your teen goes to camp or on a missions trip, write letters whenever possible. Let him know he's always on your mind.
- *Touch your encouragement.* When your teen is happy, give him a hug. When he's had a bad day, a hug, pat, or touch will reinforce the verbal encouragement.
- *Look your encouragement.* In some homes, eye contact is made only when a child is being reprimanded or given instructions. But it's also an important component of encouragement. If your words say "Good job" but your eyes say "Couldn't you do better than that?" your teen won't hear the verbal cheering.

Cheer #3: Catch Them Doing Good

One mother says, "I adored the son God gave me. He was so sweet, darling, and good-tempered—until he turned three. By the time he was four, I wondered what in the world I'd ever seen in him. My mother gave me a blank book with the instructions that every day I must record four wonderful things about my son. It didn't take long for me to again see the good in him."

Sometimes it takes extra effort to notice a teenager's

plus side, too. But it's vital to watch our kids in order to catch them doing something good or using their God-given gifts and talents—and to let them know when that happens. For example:

"I noticed that you showed mercy to your sister when you complimented her new haircut instead of making a joke about it."

"I liked the way you brought Dad the sports section of the paper this morning."

"Thanks for feeding the dog today. I appreciate it when you use your gift of service to help me."

"I saw you pick up the little boy down the street when he fell off his scooter. I can tell you care about people."

Cheer #4: Point Out the Positives

Have you noticed that it takes far more to fill our emotional bank accounts than it does to deplete them? In only a moment, a teen's fragile self-confidence can be ripped apart—even by a parent's cutting remarks.

Avoiding "self-image bombs" is a step in the right direction, but the wise cheerleader goes further. If you really want to build your teen's self-concept, try making *five positive comments for every negative remark you make*— a compliment, a word of thanks or praise or appreciation.

If you must say something negative to your teen, do so with respect, kindness, and concern. Try the "sandwich" approach, preceding and following criticism with words of love and affirmation.

Cheer #5: Let Your Teen Be an Expert

Hopefully, by the time your child is a teenager, you've helped him to identify one or more things that he can excel at and that aid him in feeling a positive sense of identity. Letting him use those talents to benefit the family is a concrete way to cheer him on.

Is your son an eagle-eyed map reader? Make him the

navigator on your next vacation. Is your daughter a math whiz? Ask her for help with your taxes.

Cheer #6: Seek Your Teen's Input

Just as teens have expertise, so they also often possess insights that could be helpful when making family decisions. Including them in that process lets them know they're needed and wanted—and gives them a chance to develop their own powers of decision making.

One couple asked their son, an electronics enthusiast, to help them decide which cordless phone to buy. Here are other examples of choices on which you might consult your teen:

- Which church to attend
- Where to go on vacation
- How to arrange living space when a grandparent comes to live with you
- What kinds of devotions would work best in your family
- Whether to repair or replace an old appliance
- What kind of family car to buy
- What to do with a tax refund
- Whether you or your spouse should accept a job offer, especially if it would require a family move.

Is Cheerleading for Everyone?

Cheering your teen on is always a challenge. For some parents, however, the challenge may seem insurmountable.

This is especially true of single parents, who often desperately need cheerleaders themselves. Yet many solo parents have discovered that cheerleading is possible—and rewarding—even when there's no squad to back them up. One single mom offers the following ideas for making it work:

- Occasionally bring a friend along when you attend your teen's events, to help ease the loneliness and the feeling of awkwardness among married parents.

- Ask friends and fellow church members to observe your teen's strengths and remind you of them.
- Don't forget God's role. Scripture says God will be "a father to the fatherless" (Psalm 68:5). It also declares, "For your Maker is your husband—the Lord Almighty is his name" (Isaiah 54:5). Remember that God cares and wants to be a parent with you.

Cheerleading: The Results

It's a rough world out there, especially for a teen with a desire to follow God. But pressing on toward the goal is a lot easier when you've got a cheering section. You can make sure your child hears and feels that priceless affirmation clearly and regularly.

steps to take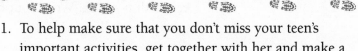

1. To help make sure that you don't miss your teen's important activities, get together with her and make a list of events (with dates and times) coming up during the next one to three months. Here are categories to get you started:

   SPORTS
   CONCERTS
   DRAMA
   AWARDS ASSEMBLIES
   RECITALS
   CHURCH EVENTS

   Ask your teen which of these events are likely to be stressful; put a star next to those and pray about them together.

2. In which of the following ways would you prefer to encourage your teen this week? Choose three; write a 1, 2, or 3 in the blank to indicate the order in which you plan to do them.

___ Face-to-face conversation

___ Phone conversation

___ E-mail

___ Letter

___ Hug

___ Gift

___ Special meal

___ Eye contact

___ Other _____

3. Can you catch your teen doing something good each day this week? It doesn't have to be something big; turning the light off when leaving her bedroom might be worth noticing. Write your observations in the spaces that follow.

SUNDAY

MONDAY

TUESDAY

WEDNESDAY

THURSDAY

FRIDAY

SATURDAY

At the end of the week, share your notes with your
teen, affirming what she did.

4. "Make five positive comments for every negative
   remark you make." Can you come up with that many
   cheers for your teen? To help you along, here are 25
   possibilities. Mark your 10 favorites; then add five of
   your own.

   ___ You are so thoughtful!
   ___ This is a tremendous improvement!
   ___ Good for you!
   ___ You are such a joy to us!
   ___ I never did that well when I was your age!
   ___ You handled that beautifully!
   ___ That's incredible!
   ___ You're really special to me—and getting more spe-
   cial every day!
   ___ I really enjoy being with you!
   ___ What a super effort!
   ___ The guy (girl) who marries you will be so lucky!
   ___ Your mom and I are so grateful to be your parents!
   ___ I really enjoy your smile!
   ___ That's fabulous!
   ___ There you go! That's it!
   ___ You're so helpful! Thank you!
   ___ You're going to make it!
   ___ I wish I could have done it that well!
   ___ I'm impressed!
   ___ I know you worked very hard on that. Wonderful
   job!
   ___ I love to hear your laugh!
   ___ I really like that!
   ___ I believe in you!

___ Excellent! That's the way to do it.
___ I love you![1]

Other _____
Other _____
Other _____
Other _____
Other _____

5. Want to affirm your teen by allowing him to be an expert? Pick one of the following tasks that fits your teen's interests and abilities—and let him do it.
___ Updating software on your computer
___ Changing the oil in your car
___ Cooking something using a recipe you've never tried
___ Redecorating a room of your home
___ Teaching you to play a video game
___ Teaching a sibling to play a sport
___ Teaching you to play a musical instrument
___ Other _____

6. In which of the following ways are you willing to seek your teen's input in order to affirm her? Check all that apply.
___ What videos to rent
___ How to landscape the yard
___ Whether to get a pet
___ How to divide the chores
___ What ministries to contribute to
___ What color to paint the house
___ How you should vote
___ Whether you should go on a diet
___ What kind of clothes you should wear
___ How to invest your money
___ Whether you should go back to school

___ What to sell in a garage sale

___ Other _____

Now underline the choice you think will confront your family next. How will you seek your teen's input on the matter?

PART 3

Helping Your Teen Make the Right Choices

9

Where to Begin: A Christian Worldview

A professor lectured at a political science class in Boulder, Colorado, where 250 students were learning the judicial history of the United States. Their minds were sharp, and they were beginning to formulate their opinions on courts, laws, attorneys, and the issues that are worth fighting for. They were ready for the professor's question: "Can any of you in this class tell me that Adolf Hitler was morally wrong by doing what he did in World War II?"

To his astonishment, not one hand went up.

He continued, "Are there any Jews in this classroom?"

One young woman on the front row raised her hand.

He walked over to her and said, "In effect, you are telling me that a man who killed six million Jewish people in one of the largest genocides in history isn't morally wrong. Are you saying you cannot find fault with a man who hung his own men by piano wire and watched them squirm while the wire slowly cut their throats? Are you telling me that a man who ordered vivisection on infants to learn how to effectively kill the human body is not morally wrong?"

She looked up at him with confidence and said, "In my opinion, what he did was wrong, but I will not stand and make a moral judgment on him."

Moral judgments in our society have become the hallmark of bad character. If someone decides to stand up for what's right, he is immediately ostracized from society and treated as if he were the cause of all the hate in the world.

Yet we must stand up and identify right from wrong. Ideas like those of Hitler have consequences.

The consequences of wrong ideas in your teen's life can be disastrous, too. A lack of standards can lead to promiscuity and abortion, drugs and other addictions, aimlessness, despair, and suicide.

Without a clear vision of the world as God made it, we are all doomed. Having a Christian worldview, however, provides that clear vision.

survey

1. **What have you done so far to teach your child a Christian worldview?**

    a. Sent him to seminary while the other kids were playing softball

b. Made sure there's a Bible under his pillow each night while he sleeps
c. Given him a brain transplant
d. Other _____

2. **You can tell whether a person sees the world through a biblical lens by**
   a. Observing whether he loves his neighbor
   b. Asking him whether Scripture is inerrant
   c. Lighting up a cigarette and seeing whether he runs away
   d. Other _____

3. **What part of a Christian worldview is hardest for you to understand?**
   a. The nature of the Trinity
   b. How theology relates to economics
   c. Whether dogs go to heaven
   d. Other _____

4. **What part of a Christian worldview would be hardest for you to instill in your teenager?**
   a. The need for evangelism in a culture of diversity
   b. The reality of spiritual warfare
   c. Not playing your Game Boy Advance in church
   d. Other _____

5. **If two Christians have different worldviews, what should they do?**
   a. Examine the Scriptures together
   b. Agree to disagree
   c. Pound each other with copies of *Strong's Exhaustive Concordance*
   d. Other _____

scripture

1. Look up Colossians 1:15-17. If everything is "held together" by Christ, what will understanding Christianity help your teen to do?

2. Read 2 Corinthians 10:5. Has your teen encountered anti-Christian arguments at school, on TV, or elsewhere? How do you know? What happened?

   Does this verse imply that we should attack those who don't have a Christian worldview? Explain.

3. Examine Matthew 22:35-37. What does it mean to love God with all your mind?

   Has the emphasis of your teen's spiritual training been on thinking or feeling? Are you satisfied with that?

4. Read Colossians 2:8. How do you suppose your teen would summarize his philosophy of life in 25 words or less? Would it depend more on human wisdom or biblical truth?

5. Look at Romans 12:2. What's one thing a parent could do to help a teen "renew" her mind?

strategies

What happens if your teen fails to develop a solid Christian worldview? He'll be stuck with the wrong map. If you try to use the wrong map, you're lost! And lost people tend to end up in dangerous neighborhoods.

When your mind goes unprotected by a comprehensive, biblical perspective, you're a sitting duck for misleading ideas that could cost you your life. At the very least, you'll end up thinking and living like those around you who are without God—instead of like a follower of Jesus Christ.

A Checklist to Get Started

Where to begin?

Here are some worldview questions you can ask your teenager right now. They'll help you grasp what kind of teachings he has been assimilating.

1. *What is God?*
a. Is there a God?
b. Is God personal or impersonal?
c. Are there many gods?
2. *What is man?*
a. Why do you wake up in the morning?
b. What are your long-term goals in life?
c. Is mankind an evolutionary step to another being?
d. Was mankind created to worship God?
3. *What is your ultimate purpose in life?*
a. Is your purpose in life to experience the most pleasure you can at all times?
b. Is your purpose in life to understand how the mind and body work together to overcome trials and struggles?
c. Is your purpose to know and serve the God of the Bible?
d. Is your purpose to be rich, powerful, or famous?

4. Where do you find truth?
a. Is truth a relative explanation of events?
b. Is truth found in yourself?
c. Is truth found in the Bible?
d. Is truth found in any other religious work as well?

The Christian Worldview

Once you've had those initial conversations to determine where your teen is, the fun really begins. Let's review several fundamental truths, or cornerstones, of a Christian worldview.

1. God is a personal being. The Christian worldview is unique: God is a real, supernatural being who desires a personal relationship with man.

When you teach kids that God is personal, it begins to open their eyes. If God is personal, they can pray to Him. They can count on Him. They begin to understand that God has their best interests in mind.

2. The breath of God formed the world. The Bible says plainly, "In the beginning God created the heavens and the earth" (Genesis 1:1). Then He made humans in His image.

If God created people, how should we deal with the issue of euthanasia? Should we intentionally kill people who no longer give anything back to society? How should we view Alzheimer's, AIDS, or any other terminal illness? As your teen grasps the concept of God's creation, she will begin to see issues like these in a new and exciting way.

3. Human nature aspires to perfection. People are attracted to what is perfect. But if your teen thinks material possessions will make his life perfect, then the latest car, the biggest house, and the most expensive toys will be his pursuit.

The Christian, however, should take on the attitude of Paul: "Not that I have . . . already been made perfect, but I press on to take hold of that for which Christ Jesus took hold of me" (Philippians 3:12).

The Christian pursues Christlikeness, which is as perfect as you can be. How would your kids' lives change if they wanted to be as perfect as Christ? What kind of movies would they watch? What would be their view of material possessions?

4. *Absolute truth is found in God.* Many people today say that ultimate truth is a figment of our imagination. The Christian worldview, on the other hand, says there is absolute, objective truth, and its source is God. First John 1:5-6 declares, "This is the message we have heard from him and declare to you: God is light; in him there is no darkness at all. If we claim to have fellowship with him yet walk in the darkness, we lie and do not live by the truth."

Some statements about God are correct; others are false. Moreover, He has created a world where some actions are clearly right and others are definitely wrong.

5. *Jesus Christ is the Son of God.* Some people call Jesus a good teacher. Some call Him a prophet. Some say He is the best example of a man who incorporated His own godhood in daily life. Scripture calls Him the Son of God. In John 8:12, Jesus said, "I am the light of the world. Whoever follows me will never walk in darkness, but will have the light of life." How many people who walk around your neighborhood claiming to be the light of the world have all their marbles?

Jesus made it even clearer to His critics when He said, "I and the Father are one." That statement was enough for them; they tried to stone Him for claiming to be God Himself (see John 10:27-33).

6. *Evil is a result of man's sin.* The apostle Paul wrote, "Sin entered the world through one man, and death through sin, and in this way death came to all men, because all sinned" (Romans 5:12).

It's important for your teen to understand that sin is a result of man's early rebellion against God. Sin was then passed from generation to generation so that the world is full of sinful people. All people try to be masters of their own lives and end up behaving in ways that disgust God.

When your teenagers grasp the consequences of sin in their lives, they will be able to appreciate the forgiveness God has offered them.

7. Jesus came to die on account of our sin and reconcile us to God. "Since death came through a man, the resurrection of the dead comes also through a man" (1 Corinthians 15:21). That man is Jesus.

The Cross is the center of the Christian faith. Jesus in all His glory decided to come down to earth to pay the penalty of sin with His own life. He reconciled us to Himself and called us to help others find Him as well.

Help your kids to understand that we are to help the pregnant teenage girl, not ostracize her. We need to bring the drunkard to the Water of Life, not send him back to death at the local bar. Jesus loved sinners of all kinds so much that He died for them.

Passing It On

Passing on a Christian worldview is not as simple as sitting your teens down for a series of lectures or family devotions. Boring your kids will hurt your cause anyway.

A far better approach is found in Deuteronomy 11:18-19: "Fix these words of mine in your hearts and minds; tie them as symbols on your hands and bind them on your foreheads. Teach them to your children, talking about them when you sit at home and when you walk along the road, when you lie down and when you get up."

Every casual dinner conversation, every movie or TV show you watch together, every drive to the store or hike in nature is rife with opportunities to discuss some aspect of the Christian worldview.

Make it a priority to reinforce the Christian worldview

with your teenagers. With that map, they will walk with God, avoid dangerous detours, and reach their destination.

steps to take

1. Try answering each of the following questions in 25 words or less.

    How do you know God really created the world?

    How do you know the Bible is true?

    How do you know that Christianity is a valid religion, and the only way to God, when the majority of the world seeks other truths and other ways?

    How do you know there is a God at all?

    Now ask your teen to answer those questions—and compare your replies. In which of these areas do you need the most help? In which does your teen need the most help?

2. If your teen asked, "Why should I care about having a Christian worldview?" which of the following answers might make the most sense to him or her?

    a. "If you're a Christian, you need a Christian world-view."

    b. "Other worldviews aren't true."

    c. "Without the right foundation, you can get into all sorts of trouble."

    d. "Because I said so."

    e. Other _____

3. How could each of the following be an opportunity to talk with your teen about having a Christian world-view?

Watching a TV news story about abortion protesters being arrested

Discovering that someone has bumped into your car in the parking lot and driven away

Receiving an unexpectedly large tax refund

Visiting your terminally ill uncle together in a nursing home

Taking a field trip to the nearest museum of natural history

4. In which of the following places are you most likely to have a chance to discuss your teen's worldview this week?

a. Going to or from church
b. At the dinner table
c. In front of the TV
d. While taking a walk
e. Other _____

5. Which of the following issues do you think you need to address first with your teen?
a. What God is like
b. God's role in the creation of the universe
c. The existence of absolute truth
d. Who Jesus is
e. People's need to be reconciled to God
f. Other _____

6. In order to address the issue(s) you just chose, how will you need to get ready?

Who (spouse, friend, pastor, etc.) could help you prepare?

10

Guiding Your Teen Toward Faith-Affirming Friendships

Mr. and Mrs. X have been living a nightmare. Both of their children have openly rebelled against the values they were taught, due in each case to the influence of a close friend.

Their 16-year-old son was the first to turn away when he became friends with a girl from a dysfunctional, non-Christian home. She told him his parents were mean, overprotective, and preventing his independence. Convinced that this girl and her single mom understood him much better than his parents did, he moved in with them! After several months and much prayer and counseling, he returned home.

Less than a year later, his sister became involved with a young man who convinced her they were in love and should live together. She abandoned her plans to attend a Christian college and moved into an apartment with the man.

Contrast those negative experiences with this one: Mr. Y's son was active in soccer. At the start of a practice, as the team was standing around talking, the conversation went downhill quickly with foul language and dirty jokes. This young man made a comment suggesting that he didn't need to hear that kind of talk and excused himself. As he walked away, he heard footsteps behind him. Another team member had joined him, saying he agreed with him. The second boy had just needed the strong influence of another to encourage him to walk away.

Friends can help keep our children on the path of righteousness—or lead them down a path of destruction.

Half of all teenagers admit that their friends influence them "a lot."[1]

Yet three-fourths still point to parents as their biggest influence.[2]

It's not too late for us to get involved by helping our teens learn how to choose friends.

survey

1. When you were growing up, you chose friends by
   a. Asking them whether they were Christians
   b. Flipping a coin
   c. Handing out dollar bills to likely prospects on the school bus
   d. Other _____

2. **Who had the strongest positive influence on you when you were a teen?**
   a. Your parents
   b. A youth worker at church
   c. The cast of *Welcome Back, Kotter*
   d. Other _____

3. **You screen your teen's friends by**
   a. Employing private detectives
   b. Using a lie detector
   c. Asking them to name the kings of Judah in alphabetical order
   d. Other _____

4. **You help your teen avoid being "unequally yoked" in dating by**
   a. Explaining the importance of shared beliefs and values
   b. Interviewing her suitors
   c. Keeping her chained in the attic
   d. Other _____

5. **Peer pressure is**
   a. A myth
   b. Unavoidable, universal, and deadly
   c. The compulsion to squint when trying to read fine print
   d. Other _____

scripture

1. Read 1 Corinthians 15:33. Has your teen ever been negatively influenced by a friend? If so, what happened?

Has your teen ever been a "bad influence" on someone else? If so, what happened?

2. Consider Proverbs 12:26. Do you feel your teen has been cautious enough in making friends so far? Why or why not?

3. Read 2 Corinthians 6:14-17. If this were the only passage in the Bible about relating to unbelievers, what would you tell your teen about having non-Christian friends?

4. Look at 1 Corinthians 5:9-13. How might this passage change your response to the previous question?

Has a *Christian* friend ever been a bad influence on your teen? If so, what did you do?

5. Read 1 Samuel 20:41-42; 23:16. What positive spiritual effect did this famous friendship have on David?

Has a friend ever had a similar influence on your teen's life? If so, how?

strategies

When our children become teens, we lose much of the control over their lives that we once had. But we can influence their choice of friends by encouraging them to become active in things that provide a positive environment, such as a sports team, youth group, or hobby club. Jim Weidmann talks about his experience as a parent:

> My wife, Janet, and I actively try to know our children's friends. We talk to our teens about who they "hang" with at school, church youth group, and sports events. We seek to understand the hot topics they're discussing. And we're very old-fashioned: We want to know where they're going, whom they're going to be with, and what time they'll be home. If they miss curfew, they know they will be grounded.
>
> I tell them I also reserve the right to show up at any place they tell me they're going. This could be a sporting event, party, or a friend's house. I don't do that out of a lack of trust, but as a loving parent who knows there are situations in a teen's life that aren't always what they seem to be. Your teen can be expecting a simple gathering with friends for a movie but have it turn out to be a beer bust in a house where no adults are present.
>
> My teens and I sometimes differ over what needs to be considered in their plans: Are the parents going to be home? Who else will be there? When is the party going to end? How will you get home? Some parents don't share your values and will actually buy alcohol and drugs for their kids. My intent is to be a safety net for my children and to provide as many ways out of any bad situation as possible.
>
> I remember when I was in high school and went to a party after a football game. I told my dad where the

party was and that the parents would be home. They were there, all right, and they bought the keg! They believed this was okay since they were there to supervise the drinking. They weren't thinking about the drive home or the other parents' values.

Well, my dad sensed something wasn't right, and he came to the party unannounced. He wanted to meet and talk with the parents. I was in the basement when someone told me my dad was upstairs. Immediately I got rid of the beer, went upstairs, and faced my dad as though nothing were wrong. I really didn't want him going to the basement! He simply told me it was time to go home.

I left with my dad. I wasn't upset, because I knew that what I had been doing was wrong. If I had told him he had embarrassed me and that I felt he didn't trust me, he would have said I was right. I had just proved I couldn't be trusted by choosing to go against our house rules. If there had been no alcohol at the party, he would have simply visited with the parents and not bothered me. As it was, he had made a strong statement to my friends, their parents, and me: He would exercise his right as my father to show up when and if he felt something was amiss. His primary goal was to protect me because he loved me.

The Yoke's on Us

The Bible tells believers not to become intimate friends with non-Christians. The apostle Paul wrote:

Do not be yoked together with unbelievers. For what do righteousness and wickedness have in common? Or what fellowship can light have with darkness? What harmony is there between Christ and Belial? What does a believer have in common with an unbeliever? (2 Corinthians 6:14-15)

Because our hearts are not one in spirit, we would be focusing on God while our friends would be focusing on the things of this world. Sin is still attractive to our old nature, and nonbelievers can persuade us to compromise our commitment, beliefs, and integrity.

This is not to say we should isolate ourselves completely from non-Christian friends. We are to share the gospel with them as we go and make disciples of all nations (see Matthew 28:18-20).

So it is with non-Christians who become our friends. We are to live in such a way that they ask why we have a joy or peace that passes all understanding. Then we're to tell them the Good News. This is known as friendship evangelism. But these are not intimate friendships or boyfriend-girlfriend relationships.

Right Relationships

What if your older teens are ready to date but don't know any Christian kids they're interested in?

In that case, wait. God is clear that we are to separate ourselves from the world while living in the world, particularly in dating.

In the meantime, encourage your children to participate in activities with other Christians. This could be in church youth groups, on a mission trip, attending teen Christian camps, or joining Christian clubs at school.

Jim Weidmann's son Jacob, 16, attends a public high school. Jacob says it's pretty obvious who is a Christian and who's not, and he chooses his close friends accordingly. The Weidmanns allow him to pick a youth group to participate in on weekends; they ask him to attend the Sunday school class at their church to see if it's engaging and spiritually challenging. If it's not, he's free to attend another church's youth group with one of his Christian acquaintances. The idea is not to exasperate him with church attendance but to have him participate weekly in developing Christian relationships.

When Friends Are Foes

What should you do when your teen is already in a relationship with a non-Christian and showing signs of bad behavior?

Your best resource is prayer. Pray that your child will see the foolishness of his friend's ways. Point out unacceptable behavior that occurs when your teen is with the other person. Use it as a warning, noting that your child is being influenced and not doing the influencing. Add that if the behavior doesn't change, you will change the situation by limiting or fully restricting the relationship.

One couple took a son out of one school and put him in another, completely cutting off all communication between the boy and a bad influence. That son is improving his grades and now has a Christian girlfriend. The family is not out of the woods, but things are a lot better than they were a year ago.

Janet Parshall, host of the *Janet Parshall's America* radio program, let her teens attend the local public high school as long at they were standing and growing in their faith. At the end of each semester, they would discuss whether they were influencing the culture or being influenced by it. A big part of this evaluation centered on whom they were hanging around with and what they were doing in their free time.

Be Intentional

There are no guarantees that our children won't rebel. But our teens will have a greater chance of walking the path of righteousness if their friends are positive rather than negative influences.

As parents, we can be intentional about guiding our teenagers into positive, God-honoring relationships.

steps to take

1. How well do you know your teen's companions? List his or her three best friends below.
   a.
   b.
   c.

   How would you describe the spiritual commitment of each of these friends?
   a.
   b.
   c.

   What additional information do you wish you had about each of these friends?
   a.
   b.
   c.

2. If you need to know more about your teen's friends, what steps will you take this week to make that happen?
   a. Ask your teen who he "hangs" with at school, church, and elsewhere
   b. Invite your teen's friends over
   c. Ask a sibling to spy on your teen
   d. Other _____

3. Which of the following statements are true of you?
   a. "When my teen goes somewhere, I know whom he's going to be with and what time he'll be home."
   ___ Always
   ___ Sometimes
   ___ Seldom
   ___ Never

    b. "I set penalties for missing curfew and make sure my
       teen knows what they are."
    ___ Always
    ___ Sometimes
    ___ Seldom
    ___ Never

    c. "My teen knows that I reserve the right to show up
       at any place he says he's going."
    ___ Always
    ___ Sometimes
    ___ Seldom
    ___ Never

4. If your teen gets into a compromising or dangerous
   situation with friends, how will he or she get out of it?
   a. Call you on the cell phone you've loaned or given
      him or her
   b. Call you on a pay phone with the money you've
      made sure he or she has
   c. Walk away and drive home in the car
   d. Other _____

   Have you discussed this plan with your teen?

   If not, when will you tell him or her about it?

5. What have you taught your teen about getting romanti-
   cally involved with non-Christians?
   a. That he should date only Christians
   b. That he can date non-Christians in order to "witness"
      to them
   c. That he can date non-Christians as long as it doesn't
      get serious

d. Nothing

e. Other _____

Are you satisfied that you've done enough in this area? Why or why not?

If you're not satisfied, what do you need to do about it this week?

6. Your teen says, "I *have* to date non-Christians. There aren't any people to go out with in our church youth group." What's your response?

   a. "Then you'll have to wait until you go to college."

   b. "You're just too picky."

   c. "Maybe you should try a different youth group."

   d. Other _____

7. The following diagram represents your teen's circle of friends. The face in the middle stands for your teen. Label the five friends with the names of five kids your teen spends time with. Then draw an arrow between your teen and each of the others to represent the influence your teen has on that friend (or vice versa). If the influence is weak, use a dotted line; if it's strong, use a thick line. If the influence is positive, draw a plus sign next to the arrow; if it's negative, draw a minus.

☺

☺   ☺

☺

☺   ☺

Now take a look at your diagram. Is there anything about these relationships that concerns you? Is there anything to be thankful for?

If a friend is negatively influencing your teen, which of the following steps do you need to take?
a. Pray
b. Warn your teen that you'll limit the friendship if the behavior doesn't change
c. Tell your teen not to spend time with that person anymore
d. Move your teen to a different school or town
e. Other _____

11

Teaching Your Teen Media Discernment

 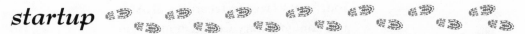

More than 40 years ago, Federal Communications Commission Chairman Newton N. Minow described American TV as a "vast wasteland." Three decades later, his concerns regarding TV were quite different. "In 1961, I worried that my children would not benefit much from television, but in 1991 I worry that my children will actually be harmed by it,"[1] he explained.

As parents who put a high premium on instilling our faith, values, and character in our young people, we should share Minow's concern about the media.

That's what Larry from Michigan sadly discovered a bit

too late. Accompanying a stack of his teen's CDs—all except one labeled with an "Explicit Lyrics" sticker—Larry wrote to *Plugged In* magazine about the struggles of dealing with a prodigal son. Larry offered this overview: "My son is hooked on this degrading, offensive music. After 14 years of Christian schooling, church, and Sunday school, he is rejecting Jesus and Christianity."

With his closing words, this father pleaded, "Please get the word out to parents before their children fall for this God-insulting music."

How can you ensure that Larry's story doesn't become your own? The first step is to understand your teen's current media diet.

survey

1. **The last time you inquired into your teen's media diet,**
   a. You were pleased with his entertainment choices
   b. You were told to submit the proper forms to his attorney
   c. Jimmy Carter was president
   d. Other _____

2. **Your teen's favorite recording artist is**
   a. A contemporary Christian musician
   b. A controversial secular singer
   c. In rehab
   d. Other _____

3. **If your teen could watch only one TV show, it would be**
   a. *Who Wants to Marry My Big, Fat Obnoxious Millionaire?*
   b. *When America's Funniest Idols Attack*
   c. Your dream come true
   d. Other _____

4. **By playing video games, your teen has learned**
   a. Outstanding eye-hand coordination
   b. How to shoot people without remorse
   c. The absolute limits of your patience
   d. Other _____

5. **When it comes to media consumption, you set the example by**
   a. Only renting G- and PG-rated videos
   b. Turning the sound down when you watch HBO
   c. Never getting extra butter on your theater popcorn
   d. Other _____

scripture

1. Look up Ephesians 5:11-12. Does your teen tend to find "the fruitless deeds of darkness" entertaining or shameful? How do you know?

2. Read Proverbs 4:15–5:6. Write down any words or phrases that remind you of current TV shows, movies, or music. Then jot down any advice you think would be worth passing on to your teenager.

3. Read Psalm 101:3. If your teen adopted this philosophy, how might it affect his viewing of TV, the Internet, video games, and films?

4. Consider Philippians 4:8. Based on this verse, what current TV show, movie, or album do you think would be worth your teen's time this week?

5. Read Psalm 1:1-4. Have you tried to replace any inappropriate parts of your teen's media diet with alternatives that emphasize "the law of the Lord?" If so, what happened? If not, do you think this is an approach worth trying?

strategies

What can you do to help your kids make better lifelong choices in entertainment?

1. Keep the main thing the main thing. Some teens—even Christian teens—willingly allow themselves to be taken "captive" by the world (Colossians 2:8). For these young people, teaching media discernment is getting the cart before the horse. What they need first is to give Jesus Christ the foremost priority in their lives.

2. Know your kids' entertainment. Find out what entertainment picks are spinning inside your teenager's head. With pen and paper and a listening ear, ask about your teen's favorite five musicians. Then list the movies and TV shows your son or daughter says are the most exciting and engaging. Follow that up by asking about his top five Internet sites. Does she go into chat rooms? If so, which ones?

Refrain from jumping in and playing judge and jury at this point. Listen, listen, and listen some more. There will be a time to offer your views, but not during this exploratory stage.

If you discover entertainment choices that concern you, schedule a follow-up time to discuss them. This will give you a chance to mull over how you're going to broach the subject (and give you time to pray).

3. Set a family standard. Each family must decide together where to draw the line, using scriptural principles as a guide. Factor in an understanding of each family member's maturity, critical thinking skills, and commitment to holiness. Don't forget prayer.

Go to great lengths, if necessary, to find common ground with your teen on media standards. Keep leading him or her back to important Bible verses and asking what conclusions he or she draws from them.

Now articulate your family's decisions in writing. Develop a "family constitution" dealing with entertainment habits in your home (see the "Steps to Take" section at the end of this chapter).

If your teen is already a fan of questionable media, you face a special challenge. You can start operating under the new standard "from this day forward," but you—and preferably your teen—must determine how to deal with the garbage festering in his or her entertainment collection. Here are some possible scenarios:

- After discovering the need for discernment, your teen may voluntarily purge the junk from his CD and movie library, as well as change his TV viewing habits.

- You can humbly accept responsibility for taking too long to "set the boundaries" and agree to replace the offenders with ones that meet the family standard.

- A local pawn shop might pay two or three bucks apiece for the discs, videos, and video games you're anxious to get rid of. Since you probably don't want to put these products back into circulation, you might agree to purchase them from your child at the same rate and then break out the sledgehammer and the Hefty bag. (Hey, they're yours now. You can do anything you want with them!)

- If you have one or two "out-of-bounds" products still in nearly new condition, you can try returning them to the store that sold them. Some retailers will refund the purchase price—or offer store credit—to a parent who makes a return because of offensive content.

After you've established family standards and weeded out everything that flunks the test, you're ready to start fresh. Hold firm to the new guidelines. From now on, if your teen asks to purchase a certain media product, you can say, "Sure, but when you bring it home, we'll review it together. If we can't agree that it meets the family standard, you'll have to get rid of it. You'll be out the money."

Rest assured: If your teen knows it's his money on the line, he'll be much more selective about which entertainers he invites home.

4. Be wary of extremes. At one extreme, some moms and dads choose to "lay down the law": No movies, no television, no secular music, period. While this approach may seem to simplify things, it may also breed rebellion if you haven't taken the time to convince your teen that it's reasonable. Young people bide their time, waiting for the day they can sample the entertainment industry's forbidden fruit: "Just wait till I move out—I'll watch and listen to whatever I want."

Other parents go to the opposite extreme, adopting an anything-goes philosophy. This permissive approach leads to "indecent exposure" as children wander, aimless and wide-eyed, through the culture's enticements.

Neither of these extremes works for most families. A discerning middle ground—one that tests entertainment against biblical standards—is the more reasonable and protective plan of action.

5. Don't judge on style or ratings. Trusting a rating system is like buying a used car solely on the basis of a classified ad that boasts, "Great car." Who decided? Based on what criteria? Though it takes a little more research, it's worth your time and effort to go beyond the rating and find out about a show's content.

Likewise, musical styles can be deceptive. While "harder" genres can offer positive messages, some mellower musicians dump lyrical sewage on their fans. Investigate the message being conveyed, not just the style or look of the messenger.

6. *Check out the ride ahead of time.* Who has time to prescreen every movie, CD, and televised program? Fortunately, there are inexpensive (sometimes free), trustworthy media-review resources that can help. *Plugged In* magazine, for example, gives concise monthly reviews of what's hot in the media. You can also reach this resource online at www.pluggedinonline.com.

7. *Ask: WWJD?* Remember the "WWJD?" bracelets that were popular several years back? While the fad may have faded, the principle behind the "What Would Jesus Do?" products will never dim. By encouraging our teens to use the "WWJD?" principle in the area of media choices, we can teach them how to fish in this media-saturated culture no matter what's on the tube, screen, radio, or CD player.

8. *Model wise choices.* One of the surest ways to derail your young person's media discernment is to act hypocritically. Nothing lasting can be accomplished if teaching discernment amounts to a parent saying, "No watching MTV in this house," while viewing *Desperate Housewives.*

9. *Don't lose hope.* Perhaps you have a teen who just doesn't get it. Don't despair. There really is hope. It may be a matter of finding the right book or tape or CD that specifically addresses today's media (for example, try the book *Mind over Media* by Stan Campbell and Randy Southern [Tyndale, 2001] and the accompanying video of

the same name). Or encourage your teen to attend a seminar on the subject at a church or youth conference.

10. *Fight the spiritual battle.* Helping our teens to have fun without being victimized by the wrong kinds of media messages doesn't just happen. It takes a "fight" to succeed. We're in a battle—a spiritual fray for the hearts and minds of our young people. Fighting for this high ground is not optional—it's essential for their well-being and protection.

Keep Treasure Hunting

Safeguarding our hearts, according to Proverbs 4:23, is something we are to strive for "above all else." This takes determined effort—a family effort. It may be painful at first, but as we continue to embrace and apply God's standards and put our potential entertainment choices under its scrutiny, we will find media discernment becoming less of a struggle and more ingrained in our nature.

steps to take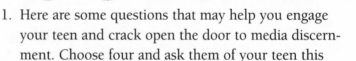

1. Here are some questions that may help you engage your teen and crack open the door to media discernment. Choose four and ask them of your teen this week after you've watched one of her favorite shows or listened together to some of her favorite music.

    ___ What is it about this form of entertainment that attracts you? Why do you like it more than others?

    ___ Why do you listen or watch? (If it's simply because friends do, ask, "Why do your friends listen to or watch it?")

    ___ How does this form of entertainment make you feel?

    ___ Do the themes reflect reality? Do they reflect truth? If they reflect reality, do they also gloss over evil?

    ___ What are the major, minor, and subtle messages being conveyed through this entertainment? Do you agree or disagree with them?

___ Do you think some people might take these messages literally? What positive things could that lead to? Negative?

___ How do the messages compare with the values you've been taught here at home or in church?

___ Do you think these messages have any effect on how close you feel to your family, friends, or God? Why or why not?

___ Would you feel comfortable if Jesus sat here listening to or watching this with you (see Matthew 28:20)? Do you think He'd be concerned, or would He enjoy it?

___ Does this entertainment reflect an opinion about God? What is it?

___ What would happen if you imitated the lifestyles and choices of the characters in these songs or this program?

___ What do you consider to be inappropriate entertainment? Where do you draw the line? Where does Scripture draw the line? Are they the same?

___ How does it make you feel to know that, by purchasing a CD, going to a movie, or watching a TV show, etc., you are supporting the ideas being promoted?

2. If your teen has inappropriate music or videos in his collection, which of the following steps will you take?

   a. Pray that he'll voluntarily purge the junk from his CD and movie library

   b. Accept responsibility for taking too long to "set the boundaries" and agree to replace the offenders with ones that meet the family standard

   c. Try to sell the products at a garage sale, on eBay, or elsewhere

d. Buy the stuff from your teen and destroy it

e. Try to return the material to the store

f. Other _____

3. Which of the following would be most helpful to your family as you make entertainment choices this week?

a. Paying more attention to movie ratings and "Parental Advisory" stickers

b. Reading reviews in *Plugged In* magazine or at www.pluggedinonline.com

c. Asking, "What would Jesus do?"

d. Getting rid of your TV set

e. Setting a family standard and putting it in writing

f. Other _____

4. Which of the following would help you become a better role model when it comes to media discernment?

a. Spending less time surfing the Internet

b. Being more careful about videos you rent or buy

c. Pointing out positive things about movies you've seen

d. Playing a different radio station in the car

e. Spending less time watching TV

f. Other _____

5. Here's a sample form you can use as a guideline to compose your own standard of what's acceptable in your home. Although it avoids the specifics, you'll want to be as specific as you can so that family members understand (and agree to) the boundaries.

Our Family Constitution for Acceptable Media
As family members committed to the lordship of Jesus Christ and wanting to live out personal holiness as He commands, we pledge from this day forward to honor God in our media choices. Despite poor decisions that

may have been made in the past, we want the blessings that come from obedience. Because we realize that certain types of entertainment are spiritually unhealthy, we ask God to guide and strengthen us as we work to make good entertainment choices, empowered by the fruit of the Spirit (self-control—our part) and the ongoing work of the Holy Spirit (His part).

Knowing that God commands us to "above all else, guard your heart" (Proverbs 4:23), we pledge to guard it from harmful influences that work against our faith.

We agree to avoid all forms of entertainment (music, film, video, Internet, magazines, books, television, video games, etc.) that _____.

In the rare event one of us feels an exception to the above should be made, we pledge to bring this issue and the possible reasons for it to the family to discuss and evaluate, rather than make this decision in isolation.

We understand that signing this "family constitution" has no bearing on our salvation (which is 100 percent dependent upon our faith in Jesus Christ as Savior and Lord), but is an outgrowth of our desire to please God and obey Him in every area of our lives. Family members sign below:

_____

_____

_____

Date _____

12

When You and Your Teen Disagree

startup

Your 16-year-old daughter is heading out the door for school wearing a skimpy tank top and jeans with holes nearly everywhere. When you question her about her appearance, she says, "Daddy, you are so old-fashioned! Everybody wears stuff like this, and I love it because it is so comfortable. See ya!"

Whether you've faced a situation like this or not, you'll inevitably find yourself in conflict with your teen. Personal preferences create some points of disagreement, while others stem from moral and safety issues. Fashion and fads may provide battlegrounds in some families, and life-and-death decisions (like drug and alcohol abuse) may invade others.

As parents, we walk a thin line between carrying responsibility for the welfare of our children and allowing that responsibility to rest on our increasingly mature young people. The lenient parent who establishes no guidelines and allows the teen to do whatever she wants runs the risk of physical danger and a loss of respect.

On the other hand, rigid, overbearing parenting can produce young adults who either rebel out of frustration or don't have enough experience and discernment to make wise decisions on their own when they arrive at maturity.

Raymond, recently graduated from college, grew up in such a home. "My parents loved me very much," he says, "but because they had been pretty wild in high school and college, they went the opposite way. My brothers and I had a strict curfew and few chances to socialize or to make our own decisions. When I went away to school, even though it was a Christian college, I was blown away by the freedom. I made some bad choices both in activities and in the company I kept. I regret some of the things I did, but fortunately I have learned from them. I've even talked my mom and dad into loosening up on my younger brothers so they'd be able to bounce those choices off [my parents] before they left home."

What should you do as a spiritual mentor when you and your teen disagree? That's what we'll explore in this session.

survey

1. When you were a teenager, you and your parents disagreed over
   a. Everything
   b. Everything except the capital of Rhode Island and the need for food

    c. Nothing, which explains why you've always doubted they were really your parents

    d. Other _____

2. **Most conflicts between parents and teens could be resolved by**
    a. Sitting down and talking things out
    b. Dr. Phil
    c. A collision between the earth and the sun
    d. Other _____

3. **A conflict is serious enough to argue over when**
    a. A moral issue is involved
    b. Your teen's health is endangered
    c. Your face turns the color of a vine-ripened tomato
    d. Other _____

4. **When it comes to hairstyles, you draw the line at**
    a. Neon colors
    b. Mohawks
    c. Head lice
    d. Other _____

5. **The ultimate goal of resolving conflict with your teen is to**
    a. Maintain the relationship
    b. Preserve the peace
    c. Save money on tranquilizers
    d. Other _____

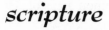 *scripture*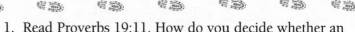

1. Read Proverbs 19:11. How do you decide whether an "offense" by your teen is too serious to overlook?

Have you ever avoided conflict by overlooking an offense by your teen, only to wish later that you hadn't? Or is the opposite more often the case?

2. Check out Proverbs 28:13. When you talk with your teen about a conflict, do you tend to admit your contribution to the problem or cover it up? If you admit it, do you usually "find mercy"?

3. Look up Philippians 2:3-4. When facing a conflict with your teen, do you make sure you understand his or her point of view? If so, how do you do it?

4. Read Matthew 7:3-5. Has your teen ever accused you during a conflict of not practicing what you preach? If so, how did you respond?

5. Examine Matthew 5:23-24. Does this passage apply only to conflicts between adults, or to those between parents and teens as well? If the latter, what should you do if you and your teen have just argued about undone homework on the way to church?

strategies

In the previous session we considered clashes over media choices. Now let's look at some other common areas of parent-teen conflict.

Earrings, Piercings, and Tattoos

Dr. Allen Johnson of the Auburn Family Institute takes a practical approach to talking with teens about piercing.

"First of all, recognize that body piercings are fads—and fads die out. Most hippies of the sixties now wear suits to their jobs. Calmly discuss the medical risks of the procedures. Navel piercing can take a year to heal, because that area is prone to infection and easily irritated by clothes. Tongues swell tremendously when first pierced and always remain tender. Improperly placed piercing, even in the cartilage of the ear, can damage nerves and cause disfigurement. Suggest temporary solutions such as faux piercings with magnetic studs."[1]

Earrings for guys may fit into the personal preference category rather than being a conflict worth battling over. They're becoming so common that some parents may choose to take their stand on other issues.

Another increasingly popular trend among teens, tattooing, can also create conflict. Try to get your youngster to see things from a long-range view. What would your son's future wife think about that heart on his shoulder (especially if it contains someone else's initials)? Tattoos also involve medical risk, including increased possibilities of contracting hepatitis B, HIV, or tetanus from the needles and dyes.

Clothing and Hairstyles

How do you guide your teen toward appropriate (and affordable) clothing and hairstyles?

Common sense and clear communication are the keys. At times the hole-filled jeans may drive us crazy, but come back to this question: Is it worth arguing over?

One mom stated, "Our rule was that as long as the clothing was not immodest, indecent, or vulgar, it was their choice. . . . But the call on immodesty came down to Mom, not to them."

Sit down with your teen and discuss what clothes say to others. If you wear a shirt that has the name of a particular band or product (beer, for example) on it, will people think you are endorsing it?

Then there's the "need" many feel to have name-brand clothing. Some parents establish what they think is a reasonable clothing allowance and then allow their teens to make their own decisions. This involves a little risk, but encourages a long-range view.

When it comes to hairstyles, how critical are they? A good question to ask is, "What is the young person communicating, or trying to?" That can serve as the foundation for a meaningful conversation.

A mom said, "Who really cares if their hair is shaved funny or dyed a pretty color that you only see on rainbows? I'd rather have my kid come home with hair that makes me cringe than to rebel through the use of drugs. The rule I've had in our house is that I will pay for a standard haircut, but anything else comes out of their own pockets."

Curfews

When discussing a curfew, help your teen to see the big picture—to consider how busy his weekly schedule is, how challenging it is to get him up in the morning, what his plans are for the following day, and who is doing the driving.

One family developed a rolling pattern based on the age of the children. The mom said, "In ninth grade, the curfew was 11:00 P.M. as long as there was no school the next day. The time advanced a half hour each successive year. There were some special-event curfews that varied from that, but there was always a curfew of some kind."

What happens if curfew is violated? The response should be based on the circumstances and on the teen's attitude.

As with other areas of conflict, parents need to keep in mind that curfews are not ends in themselves, but part of the overall parenting package. When you establish a curfew, remind your teen that it's in her own best interest.

Drugs and Alcohol

Dealing with these issues will be far easier if you've built a good relationship, with clear and honest communication, before the temptations arise. Talk to your children about the effects of drugs and alcohol and about the loss of control experienced by those who use them. Encourage them to communicate with you when they're confronted with the possibility of using drugs or drinking alcohol.

Scripture clearly speaks about avoiding drunkenness. Whatever your family rules about drinking, remember how important your example is for your teen. If he sees you drinking when you've said he shouldn't, or abusing alcohol by drinking to excess, he has little incentive to follow any more-restrictive guidelines you might choose to set on him.

Don't assume that because your teen attends a Christian school or is home-schooled, he will not be approached or tempted by such activity. Pay attention to changes of behavior, and don't hesitate to be involved in decisions for her welfare. Observe the friends with whom she associates.

If your child does become involved in drug or alcohol abuse, demonstrate the type of tough love that can draw him out of the pattern without destroying the relationship. Depending on the severity of the situation, intervention or treatment may be necessary. Trust has been broken, but unconditional love and forgiveness can go a long way if the teen is willing to turn from the destructive lifestyle.

Boyfriends and Girlfriends

For families who see dating as an option (as opposed to those who favor a courtship model), you want your child to date people who will provide a positive relationship. But your opinion of desirable qualities may differ from your teen's.

If possible, establish guidelines well before the

question of dating arises in your family. Some parents set a particular age or grade as a prerequisite; others may tie the opportunity to a specific event. If a special dating relationship develops, the same guidelines hold as in other potential conflict arenas: Pay attention, communicate, be involved, and don't overreact.

Discuss the concept of setting limits in any dating situation at the beginning. Establish specific guidelines, such as avoiding situations in which the couple is alone together behind closed doors. By having this conversation before a relationship begins, you empower your teen to hold fast to boundaries and to show respect for his date by communicating them early.

Get to know the person your child is dating. A reasonably protective nature may cause some disagreements. You may have a greater tendency to show this level of concern for daughters than for sons, but parents of boys should also make the effort to get to know the girls their sons are dating.

Finally, avoid the temptation to overreact and yank in the leash. Putting your daughter in an "us vs. him" situation rarely leads to the desired end.

Choosing Your Battles Carefully

Every family has to choose its own issues that are worth fighting over, and these issues may even vary between different children from the same household. For some, movie choices may be battlegrounds; others may want to draw a line in the sand over music selection.

But remember that discernment is the ultimate goal in dealing with these issues. As parents, we can't and shouldn't make every decision for our children throughout their lives; we must use these situations to help them develop critical thinking skills and awareness enough to make wise choices on their own.

steps to take

1. Here are two real-life memories students have of conflicts with their parents.

   a. "After my freshman year of college, I decided that I wanted to take some time off from school. Of course my parents didn't agree, but instead of simply telling me what to do, they encouraged me to seek God's will in the situation and supported me in whatever decision I came to."

   How is this approach similar to the way you've been handling conflict with your teen? How is it different?

   Is there anything in this story that might help you in a parent-teen disagreement you're facing? Explain.

   b. "There were no ducks that morning. We sat cold and shivering in the duck blind. After a night of fierce debate, we didn't feel like saying much. Dad is the most wise man I know, but at that time I was less than impressed. I felt like Dad had no clue what I was feeling. When he broke the silence, I braced myself for lecture #101. He proceeded to explain exactly how I felt. He shared a similar experience he had when growing up. He told me he loved me and that it was his job as a parent to offer guidance in my life. When all was said and done, I felt a total peace. I knew I was loved and was reassured that he had my best interest at heart. He understood me yet still held on to what he thought was best. His excellent parenting directed me straight into God's will."

How is this approach similar to the way you've been handling conflict with your teen? How is it different?

Is there anything in this story that might help you in a parent-teen disagreement you're facing? Explain.

2. In which of the following areas are you facing conflict with your teen these days? Choose all that apply.
   a. Earrings, piercings, or tattoos
   b. Clothing or hairstyles
   c. Curfews
   d. Drugs or alcohol
   e. Boyfriends or girlfriends
   f. Music or other media
   g. Other _____

3. When you try to handle these conflicts, which of the following tends to be your downfall?
   a. Being too harsh
   b. Being too lenient
   c. Lacking time or energy
   d. Panicking
   e. Trying to do things without God's help
   f. Other _____

4. Based on your previous answer, which of the following do you need most this week?
   a. Gentleness
   b. Courage
   c. To examine your priorities
   d. Patience

e. Prayer

f. Other _____

5. Which of the following skills do you most need to
   develop in order to resolve conflict with your teen?
   a. Listening
   b. Setting clear boundaries
   c. Enforcing boundaries
   d. Negotiating
   e. Other _____

   Do you know anyone (friend, relative, pastor) who's
   good at the skill you named in the previous question?
   If so, when could you ask that person to give you
   some tips?

6. Think about a battle you tend to have with your teen.
   Into which of the following categories does it fall?
   a. Not really worth the energy we've put into it
   b. Worth discussing, but not fighting over
   c. Worth a confrontation, even if it's uncomfortable
   d. Worth a major, ongoing war

7. Based on your previous answer, which of the following
   steps should you take this week to resolve the conflict?
   a. Let it go
   b. State my position, then let it go
   c. Work toward a compromise
   d. Explain why I can't compromise
   e. Other _____

PART 4

Discipling
Day by Day

13

Creating an "Eager Learner" Attitude

You may be ready, even eager, to help your teen grow spiritually. But you're not the only part of the equation. Your teen must be ready, too.

Steven is a case in point. He prayed to receive Christ in early elementary school, and his parents made sure he was in church every Sunday. They taught him to pray at bedtime and meals; they bought him Bibles; they had family devotions whenever they could. They did their best to let Steven know that they loved him, to teach him right from wrong, and to follow Christ consistently themselves.

But Steven had problems. He struggled in school. He

made some less-than-desirable friends. When adolescence hit, he tried marijuana. Soon he was a regular user. Later he began to drink, and he eventually became an alcoholic. Steven's parents were devastated. No matter how much they tried to "water" their son, he seemed unable or unwilling to grow spiritually.

Steven wasn't ready.

Like many teenagers, Steven found himself in the grip of habits and hurts that kept him from making spiritual progress. Thankfully, through God's grace and the help of wise counselors as well as his persistent parents, Steven has begun to get his life back on track as an adult.

He bears the scars of those turbulent years, however. His parents do, too, no doubt wondering what they could have done to prevent the "waste" of Steven's adolescence.

Your son or daughter may not be burdened by problems like Steven's, but it doesn't take dramatic conflicts and addictions to keep a teen from being an eager spiritual learner. Sometimes seemingly small, unresolved issues can stall the discipling process.

The good news is that those issues aren't a mystery. In this session we'll look at how to deal with them.

survey

1. **Your teen's readiness to grow spiritually is like**
   a. A flower's eagerness for water
   b. A kitten's eagerness for catnip
   c. A toddler's eagerness for Brussels sprouts
   d. Other _____

2. **Your teen's spiritual progress is sometimes blocked by**
   a. Low self-esteem
   b. Problems in your relationship

    c. Your youth pastor's insistence on wearing a clown
       suit

    d. Other _____

3. **Your teen might be more eager to learn if you would**
    a. Show more unconditional love
    b. Be a better listener
    c. Stop running over his skateboard with your car
    d. Other _____

4. **Spiritually speaking, your teen has been most successful in**
    a. Sharing his faith
    b. Having regular devotions
    c. Eating pizza at retreats
    d. Other _____

5. **You help your teen dream of new possibilities by**
    a. Introducing him to Christians who do innovative
       things
    b. Asking him what he'd like to do with his life
    c. Poking him with a sharp stick
    d. Other _____

scripture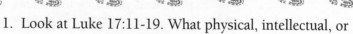

1. Look at Luke 17:11-19. What physical, intellectual, or emotional need did Jesus meet here?

As a result, how was the leper freed to make spiritual progress?

2. Read John 4:10-18, 25-29. What physical, intellectual, or emotional need did Jesus meet here?

As a result, how was the woman freed to make spiritual progress?

3. Consider Luke 19:2-10. What physical, intellectual, or emotional need did Jesus meet here?

As a result, how was Zacchaeus freed to make spiritual progress?

4. Read Mark 8:1-8. What physical, intellectual, or emotional need did Jesus meet here?

As a result, how was the crowd freed to make spiritual progress?

strategies

Experienced youth mentors have identified seven factors that make the difference between the spiritually ready and the resistant. How can you make sure these factors are present in your teen's life? Let's find out.

Factor #1: Showing Unconditional Love

It's easy for kids to get the idea that if they don't measure up, they don't earn love—or at least not enough of it. When spiritual growth is what's being measured, the problem is no less real. *If I try to memorize a chapter of the Bible and can't do it, my parents will be disappointed. If*

I admit that I have doubts about God, my parents will be mad.

The result: Kids don't attempt the Scripture memory program for fear of failure. They keep their doubts a secret, and their unanswered questions become time bombs that explode when they get to college.

How can you make sure your teen really knows you love him or her—with no fine print?

- Say it, even if it seems obvious.
- Don't stop with words.
- Don't save love for special occasions.
- Keep your teen's emotional tank full.
- Hate the sin, but love the sinner.

Factor #2: Demonstrating Visible Grace

The parent who extends God's grace to a teen opens up a world of possibilities. By setting aside the past, that mom or dad permits a future.

A home without grace, on the other hand, stifles spiritual growth. Picture 16-year-old Max, whose father has a photographic memory for every sin Max has ever committed. Max's dad never misses a chance to bring up these "ongoing problems" as exhibits A through Z in what seems to Max like an endless criminal trial.

If Max is wrestling with a "secret" sin that he needs to get beyond in order to grow, is he likely to confess it to Dad? Will Max even be *interested* in "growing" in order to resemble his "spiritual," quick-to-condemn father?

Grace usually makes the giver and the receiver feel better. But for those of us who want to guide our teens, it does far more. It clears the way for spiritual growth.

Factor #3: Disciplining Effectively

You may be wondering: *What does the way I discipline my teenager have to do with his or her spiritual growth?*

Here are four answers:

1. The way you discipline can shape the way your teen thinks and feels about God.

2. A teen who's allowed to defy parents probably will reject God's authority as well.

3. Kids without boundaries often fall into activities that distract them from following Jesus.

4. The goal of discipline is to help kids develop self-discipline, a quality vital to discipleship.

Here are four ways to practice the kind of discipline that helps a teen become an eager spiritual learner:

1. Show mercy as well as firmness.

2. Don't relinquish your parental authority too soon.

3. Limit time-wasting activities as well as banning dangerous ones.

4. Think long-term by helping your teen develop self-discipline.

Factor #4: Seeing the Possibilities

The child who sees only what *is* can't envision what *could be*. How can you help your teen see exciting possibilities in his or her spiritual future? Here are a few ideas:

1. *Encourage exploration.* From time to time ask your teen, "What activities do you like the most these days? Can you think of any ways to serve God through them?"

2. *Welcome a desire to help others.* When teens lift their eyes from daily concerns and notice the needs of people around them, many are spurred to think of ways to help.

3. *Supply examples.* Simply spending time around adults who serve God in a variety of ways can get kids thinking about their own goals.

Factor #5: Seeing Results from Personal Accomplishments

We need successes, not failures, to keep us going. The guy who asks 12 friends to a Christian concert and gets 12 turndowns isn't likely to ask number 13.

Kids need to see that their efforts make a difference. They need "success experiences" like these:

- *I prayed that God would help me make friends, and He did.*
- *I gave money for hunger relief, and I got a letter back from a little boy who was helped.*
- *I told a girl at school about Jesus, and she listened without laughing at me.*

You can't insulate your teen from failure, but you can increase the chances that his effort will yield positive results. Here's how:

1. *Make sure he is prepared.*

2. *Aim for realistic goals.*

3. *Explain that results aren't always visible, predictable, or instantaneous.*

4. *When a project goes wrong, talk about it.*

5. *Follow up.* When possible, help your teen find out how his effort made a difference. Not every accomplishment will have measurable results, but those that do will be a special encouragement to your teen.

Factor #6: Celebrating Achievements

Parents who show appreciation for their child's accomplishments are setting the stage for bigger and better things. That's true for significant moments in a child's spiritual growth, too.

How can you recognize and reward your teen's spiritual progress? Here are three ideas to get you started.

1. If you've been asking your teen to change a particular behavior (griping about going to church, for example), thank him when he does.

2. Ask your teen's opinion about a spiritual matter into which she has recently shown insight. If she's demonstrated discernment in choosing her music or TV shows, for instance, ask her to critique a song or program you like.

3. When you spot your teen acting as a servant to someone else, volunteer to be her servant for an hour.

Factor #7: Unloading Psychological Baggage

Nothing puts the brakes on a teen's spiritual growth quite like dragging around the baggage of guilt, shame, fear, and indecision. If 17-year-old Andy feels ashamed because he's addicted to Internet porn, no one will be able to convince him that spending more face-to-face time with God is a good idea.

How can you help your teen get rid of emotional burdens? You can start by learning to ask three key questions, as veteran youth worker and speaker J. David Stone has pointed out:

1. What's wrong?
2. How do you feel?
3. What are you doing?

The first time you ask those three questions, the answers may not be long. Be patient.

To bring closure to your conversation, try asking, "What do you need to do to get what you want?" If you've worked through the three questions, it's likely that your teen will already have some ideas. If not, you can offer advice. Either way, pray with your child, and help him come up with a plan of action.

When that happens, you're clearing the path to spiritual progress. Unloading psychological baggage enables your child to return to a learning mode. That's when she's ready to grow again.

steps to take

1. If your teen admitted that he no longer believed everything in the Bible, you would
   a. Say, "Yeah, neither do I"
   b. Scream and pass out

c. Send him away to boarding school

d. Affirm your unconditional love for him and offer to explore his questions together

e. Other _____

2. If your teen totaled his car during a snowstorm but escaped without injury, you would

a. Buy him a new car and say, "I'm just thankful you didn't get hurt"

b. Bring the incident up every day for the rest of your life

c. Inflict a few injuries yourself

d. Demonstrate visible grace by reviewing how to drive on snow but not dredging up the incident again

e. Other _____

3. If your teen told you she was going to study with a friend but went to see a movie instead, you would

a. Forbid her to see the friend again

b. Forbid her to see a movie again

c. Ignore the whole thing

d. Discipline her lovingly but effectively by grounding her for a week, talking about honesty, and assuring her of your continuing affection

e. Other _____

4. If your teen felt like a failure because he got cut from the basketball team, you would

a. Make him wear a tutu to school

b. Tell him to quit moping and get over it

c. Say, "I guess you're no better at sports than I am"

d. Help him see the possibilities by reminding him how Michael Jordan was cut from his junior high basketball team before going on to stardom

e. Other _____

5. If your teen wanted to keep her faith a secret because someone laughed at her for saying grace in the school cafeteria, you would
   a. Let her off the hook by saying, "That's okay, no need to look like a religious nut"
   b. Condemn her by saying, "If you're ashamed of the gospel, I'm ashamed of you"
   c. Make her feel guilty by saying, "Do you want your friends to end up in hell?"
   d. Remind her of the results of her accomplishments by saying, "But remember how you invited your friend Carole to the church lock-in and didn't get laughed at?"
   e. Other _____

6. If your teen decided to start having a personal devotional time and stuck with it for six months, you would
   a. Not mention it in case your attention would cause her to lose interest
   b. Grumble that she was trying to make you look bad
   c. Warn her that she'd better keep it up for at least a year
   d. Celebrate her achievement by throwing a little "anniversary party" at the dinner table
   e. Other _____

7. If your teen didn't want to go to a youth retreat and just shrugged sadly when you asked why, you would
   a. Say, "When I ask you a question, I expect an answer"
   b. Shrug back and let the matter drop
   c. Order him to go anyway
   d. Unload his psychological baggage by asking, "What's wrong?"
   e. Other _____

8. Based on your answers to the previous questions, which of the following do you think you most need to work on this week?
   a. Showing unconditional love
   b. Demonstrating visible grace
   c. Disciplining effectively
   d. Seeing the possibilities
   e. Seeing results from personal accomplishments
   f. Celebrating achievements
   g. Unloading psychological baggage

9. Which of the following might keep you motivated to work on the factor you just named?
   a. Envisioning your teen at his next stage of spiritual growth
   b. Fearing the ridicule of other parents at church
   c. The prospect of the Lord telling you someday, "Well done"
   d. Knowing that time is running out
   e. Other _____

14

Ideas for Raising a Faithful Follower

Author and educator Eugene Peterson once published a book on discipleship titled *A Long Obedience in the Same Direction*. That intriguing phrase captures what all Christian parents hope their teen will achieve—a lifelong obedience to Christ. A steady march in the direction of holiness and godliness. A persistent, vibrant faith that can't be held back.

Think for a moment about the apostle Paul. Even a quick reading of his New Testament letters reveals a man of single-minded determination. He had a firm sense of mission, and would not let diversions and distractions deter from an all-out pursuit of his goal:

"One thing I do: Forgetting what is behind and straining toward what is ahead, I press on toward the goal to win the prize for which God has called me heavenward in Christ Jesus" (Philippians 3:13-14).

At this stage of your life, what is the "one thing" you do? What is the one thing that compels you, motivates you, and excites you more than anything else?

Consider the idea of making the nurturing of your teen's faith your *one thing*. During the brief, swiftly passing years when your teen is accessible and responsive to your influence, set as your number-one goal helping your son or daughter become a true, genuine disciple of Christ.

survey

1. **Your number-one goal for the next year is**
   a. To inspire your teen to become an on-fire follower of Jesus
   b. To fan the feeble flame of faith in your teen's heart
   c. To keep yourself from spontaneously combusting
   d. Other _____

2. **You'll know your teen is a true disciple when he**
   a. Asks himself, "What would Jesus do?"
   b. Grows a beard and wears sandals
   c. Sends e-mails in King James English
   d. Other _____

3. **The best "teachable moments" you've had with your teen were**
   a. At bedtime and at meal times
   b. In the car and in the kitchen
   c. Under protest and under duress
   d. Other _____

4. **To find another spiritual mentor for your teen, you would look for**
   a. Maturity
   b. Enthusiasm
   c. Someone with time on his hands
   d. Other _____

5. **The best time to talk with your teen about spiritual things is**
   a. Right after school
   b. Right after a disappointment
   c. Right after giving him his allowance
   d. Other _____

scripture

1. Read Proverbs 27:17. Has interacting with a mentor or friend ever "sharpened" your commitment as a follower of Jesus? If so, how?

   If you've tried to mentor your teen spiritually, have you and he sharpened each other or just rubbed each other the wrong way? Explain.

2. Consider Galatians 6:2. Which of the following might be slowing down your teen's spiritual growth: (a) a chore or job that keeps him from spending time in the Bible or with other Christians, (b) an emotional weight (guilt, low self-esteem) that discourages him from approaching God or trying new things, or (c) stress that steals his energy and preoccupies his thoughts?

How could you help carry that burden?

3. Look up James 5:16. Have you ever confessed a sin to your teen? If so, what happened? If not, why not?

Have you ever asked your teen to pray for you? If so, what happened? If not, why not?

4. Read 1 Corinthians 4:14-16; 11:1. Would you feel comfortable making statements like these to your teen? Why or why not?

What's one way in which you're trying to follow Christ's example?

Has your teen seen you doing that? If so, what happened? If not, why not?

strategies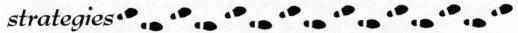

Here are a dozen ideas to help you guide your teen to an authentic faith.

#1: *Teachable Moments*

Take advantage of everyday opportunities: driving to school and soccer practice, working together around the house. At times like these, you can talk with your teen about life and love, faith and the future.

To make the most of the moment, don't give a sermon; tell about your own life. Be on the lookout for lessons waiting to happen. TV commercials, songs on the radio, news events, reminders of mistakes you made as a teen—all these provide grist for discussion.

#2: *"Bookend" Your Teen's Day*

Joe White took literally the admonition in Deuteronomy 6: "Talk [with your children] when you lie down and when you get up" (verse 7). As much as his schedule (and his kids' activities) allowed, he would begin each day with morning devotions with his kids, and he would end each day by lying down on their beds at night to talk, pray, and memorize Scripture together.

Will most parents be able to have morning devotions with their kids *and* "lay-by" time in the evening? If you can't do both, pick one or the other—and stick with it. Use those times to pray together, read Bible passages, memorize verses, and talk about life.

#3: *Small-Group Study with Friends*

For 12 years, Bill Slocum has led Bible study/accountability groups for teens. "Those kids pray for one another and encourage one another," Bill says. "Most of the time, I just provide the kitchen table and a box of donuts—the boys keep the group going because they want it and need it."

Few activities will keep your teen growing in his faith more than involvement with a small group of like-minded Christians. Do everything you can to encourage your child to find a Bible study or discipleship group to meet with weekly.

If all else fails, take a page out of Bill Slocum's play book: Launch a group of your own.

#4: *Church and Youth Group Participation*

Teens need to be involved with other students in fellowship, teaching, service, and good, clean fun. Being involved in a strong church youth program provides teens (and their parents) many benefits, including:

1. A positive alternative to negative environments.

2. A network of Christian friends and peers.

3. A chance to be part of something "bigger than themselves."

4. The reinforcement of values from people besides Mom and Dad.

#5: *Connect Your Teen to a Christian Mentor*

At some point, your teen will assert his independence. He won't seek your input; he'll look to other people for affirmation and guidance.

Wise parents see this scenario coming—and plan for it by enlisting the help of other mentors. If you're fortunate, your church may have a mentoring program. If not, here are a few suggestions for locating a mentor:

1. Pray.

2. Explore your network of friends, relatives, and church members.

3. Seek and you just may find.

#6: *Hold a Blessing or Rite of Passage Ceremony*

The point of these events is to honor your child and reinforce the ideals you've been teaching. Here are two examples:

1. *A blessing ceremony.* This could range from the very simple (a few people praying over your teen before he

leaves for college) to the sophisticated (a meal, a formal blessing, prayers, gifts).

2. *A manhood/womanhood ceremony.* This event highlights a milestone in a teen's journey toward adulthood (for instance, age 13, 16, 18—or all of them). It might take place at a conference center, a restaurant, or your home. It might involve your immediate family, a handful of friends and family members, or a large number of people.

#7: Teach the Importance of Evangelism

Does your teen know the importance of telling people about God's love and grace? You can model for your teen a concern for the lost *and* some kind of active witness to them.

Your teen needs to know that there are hundreds of ways to let his light shine. Some people have the ability and boldness to approach people on campus and tell them about Jesus. Others might feel more comfortable inviting a friend to a concert at church. Still others do best at witnessing by serving others.

#8: Show Your Teen How to Disciple Friends

Discipling someone is a great way for your teen to grow and develop his own faith. As the saying goes, "No one learns more than the teacher."

If your teen expresses an interest in discipling someone, or if you want to encourage him in this direction, keep in mind a few points:

1. A goal of discipleship is to help all involved—but especially the less-mature believer—to grow in knowledge and understanding of Christ, to develop his faith, and to make steps toward Christlikeness.

2. This kind of relationship can be one-on-one or in a group setting.

3. Lead and encourage your teen by example. It will send a powerful message if your son or daughter sees you

meeting with someone in a discipling role and hears you talk about how rewarding it is.

#9: *Continually Cast a Vision for Sexual Purity*

The best way you can instill in your teen a sense of purity's importance is to model it. This means being cautious about what you allow into your own mind via the Internet, television, and other sources.

Use teachable moments to discuss sexuality. You're bound to see TV commercials or billboards with suggestive messages. Take the opportunity to talk about them.

Reinforcing the importance of sexual purity is an ongoing process. Some parents are eager to get the "sex talk" out of the way and leave that awkward subject alone. But you need to have an open-ended, running dialogue with your teen.

#10: *Cultivate Peacemaking Skills*

Jesus singled out people with this quality for special recognition: "Blessed are the peacemakers, for they will be called sons of God" (Matthew 5:9).

Teens need to learn how to promote harmony at school, on the job, and at church; resolve disagreements with friends and family members; work together with people they find irritating; and defuse tense situations. Peacemaking is an essential part of Christian life and witness to the world.

Does your teen have these skills? If so, cultivate and honor them. If not, work on helping him or her develop in this area.

#11: *Help Your Teen Learn Respect and Reverence for God*

Where will teens learn to revere God? Two places, primarily:

1. Home. If you treat your relationship with God and the Bible in a cavalier manner, you're likely to find your teen doing the same. Consider how you talk to God—and how you respond when someone uses His name in vain. Do you sit passively through movies or TV shows that belittle His authority?

2. Church. Sadly, some churches seem to present God as a buddy. While it's true that God desires friendship with us, there's a danger in trying to bring Him down to our level. What attitude toward God does your teen pick up in your church?

#12: Instill a Heart for Missions and Service

Help your teen develop a global missions perspective. How?

1. Read missionary biographies.
2. Attend missionary meetings.
3. Have missionaries in your home.
4. Become pen pals with missionaries or their children.
5. Send a care package to a missionary.
6. Adopt a national—a child or a pastor.
7. Take a missions trip.
8. Pray for missionaries.[1]

Encourage your teen to see that God is at work throughout the world, and that she can be a part of the exciting things happening through missions—abroad *and* at home.

steps to take

Here are 10 real-life stories in which students remember how their parents discipled them. After each story, indicate whether you'd like to adapt the activity for use with your teen, and what kinds of changes you might make in the approach.

1. "My mom and I had many late-into-the-night discussions while sitting on my bed. She was not afraid to answer any of my questions, and no concern or frustration was too silly for her. She laughed with me, cried with me—she made me feel valuable by just wanting to be with me. These times laid a foundation of trust that made me want to ask about more spiritual matters."

___ I'd like to adapt this activity for use with my teen.

Here's how I might do it:

2. "Before I got my driver's license, Daddy used to drive me about 10 minutes to school every morning. During this time we would listen to Chuck Colson's 'Breakpoint' commentary on the radio and then discuss the day's topic/issue. These times helped me begin to understand the importance of having a Christian worldview, and I saw my daddy's passion for God's truth and how that relates to our culture."

___ I'd like to adapt this activity for use with my teen.

Here's how I might do it:

3. "My Dad and I would read Scripture, usually Proverbs, before I went to school in junior high. This kept me floating during a period when I was lukewarm in my Christian life."

___ I'd like to adapt this activity for use with my teen.

Here's how I might do it:

4. "During high school, Dad and I would often eat breakfast together at our kitchen table, and we'd sometimes talk about spiritual questions I had. My favorite part, which encouraged me most, was when we ended that time in prayer. It really prepared me for the day."

___ I'd like to adapt this activity for use with my teen.

Here's how I might do it:

5. "My mom and I had long conversations in her room at night before bed. These 'debriefing' conversations not only allowed me to share my heart and struggles with her, but they also allowed her to give me guidance and the assurance that she was always there to encourage as I tried to be a godly teen. The culmination of these times—the laughter, tears, and times of conflict—created an impenetrable bond between us."

___ I'd like to adapt this activity for use with my teen.

Here's how I might do it:

6. "In middle school, my parents were separated for a while. My mom encouraged my brother and sister and me to memorize a passage to help us through that time. Jeremiah 29:11-15 is still my favorite passage."

___ I'd like to adapt this activity for use with my teen.

Here's how I might do it:

7. "My mom was continually, and still is, involved in guiding me in my dating life. She would always tell me she was praying for my relationships, and she always made an effort to know my 'significant other.' That meant a lot and showed me that she was interested in my life not only then, but also that she was interested in my future happiness."

___ I'd like to adapt this activity for use with my teen.

Here's how I might do it:

8. "From the time I was in fourth or fifth grade until I was in high school, Dad and I would get up at 6:00 and read to each other from a book called *Character Sketches,* which took a character trait and showed how it was present in the life of an animal and a biblical character. These special times taught me how important a daily time with the Lord is. I will always treasure them because they belonged to only Dad and me—no one else. I had his undivided attention."

___ I'd like to adapt this activity for use with my teen.

Here's how I might do it:

9. "My mom did not like to cook much, but when she did I would go in the kitchen with her and talk. We would share so much about our lives, talking very openly and relating as friends. This didn't occur until I was going through adolescence and I was able to appreciate all she had given to me and to accept her unconditionally. Now she is my best friend."

___ I'd like to adapt this activity for use with my teen.

Here's how I might do it:

10. "Because I didn't have my own car during high school, my parents drove me everywhere—to youth group, baseball practice, friends' houses. I remember that they really tried to use that time—whether it was a five-minute drive or an hour—to talk about things. They could have turned on the news or a game, or stayed in their own world like we all do sometimes when driving. But they always made an effort to ask questions and draw me out. If I was coming home from Bible study, Mom would say, 'What did you learn? What do you think about that?' If I was coming home from school, Dad would say, 'Tell me about your friends' or 'What can I be praying about in your life?' Recently, I asked my folks about all those drive-time discussions, and they said, 'We decided early on that if we

were going to spend hours each week driving you around, it was going to be time well spent.' And it sure was. I stayed connected to my parents talking during all those hours in the car."

___ I'd like to adapt this activity for use with my teen.

Here's how I might do it:

15

Never Quit on a Child

Is there a surefire recipe for raising well-adjusted, responsible, and conscientious teenagers? Probably not. But as Joe White discovered, there *is* an essential ingredient that no successful parent can do without:

> My father, now in his eighties, has always been a man of simple faith, sure convictions, and straightforward speech. He's also one of the wisest people I know. When I visited him one time, I asked, "Dad, what would you say is the key to successful parenting?"
>
> He squinted his green eyes and wrinkled his brow, then said, "Relentlessness."
>
> I waited a moment to see if he might elaborate, but

he just stared at me as if his one-word answer needed no further explanation.

Finally, I pressed for more. "So, what exactly does that mean to you?"

He ran a rough hand over his whiskers and pushed back the cap he was wearing. "Relentlessness," he said, "you know, tenacity, stubbornness, perseverance, persistence. It means when your 16-year-old smashes up your brand new pickup, you hug him and tell you did the same thing when you were his age. It means when your daughter tells you she hates you, you tell her, 'I'll always love you.' It means that when your son makes some boneheaded decision, you stand by him and support him through all the consequences. Basically, relentlessness means that you never, ever give up on your kid."

As a father who had guided two children through the teen years at that time—with another two in the midst of them—I knew exactly what Dad meant and I knew how right he was. So many times I've wanted to just let my kids "do their own thing" because my parenting strategies weren't working. But I didn't. I acknowledged where I had failed and redoubled my efforts to improve.

So many times I've wanted to say "See, I told you so!" when one of my teens ignored my advice and ended up in a mess. But I didn't. I held my tongue and simply listened without judgment as my son or daughter poured out his or her heart to me.

So many times I've wanted to give up because I was tired or frustrated or disappointed. But I didn't. I prayed for strength, reached deep within myself, and summoned the determination to do the best I could for my teenagers.

There may be a lot of things that go into effective, successful parenting, but right at the top of the list is the word *relentlessness*.

survey

1. **What did you do as a teenager that most exasperated your parents?**
   a. Put frogs in the dresser drawers and short-sheeted the beds
   b. Burned your neighborhood to the ground
   c. Refused to leave home, where you live to this day
   d. Other _____

2. **When have you felt like giving up on your teen?**
   a. When he didn't want to go to church
   b. When he created a computer virus that brought the world to the brink of thermonuclear war
   c. Only on days with the letter "Y" in them
   d. Other _____

3. **What has kept you from giving up on your teen?**
   a. Love
   b. Legal ramifications
   c. Loss of short-term memory
   d. Other _____

4. **What do you think would happen if you gave up on your teen?**
   a. You would be wracked with guilt
   b. She would end up living in a cardboard box
   c. Let's find out, shall we?
   d. Other _____

5. **What do you think has kept God from giving up on you?**
   a. His mercy
   b. His compassion
   c. His sense of humor
   d. Other _____

scripture

1. Read Luke 15:11-24. If you were the prodigal son's father, how long do you think you might have waited before giving up on the boy?

   Would it be harder for you to keep hoping and praying for a rebellious teen or to welcome him when he returned? Why?

2. Look at Galatians 6:9. What three parts of parenting a teen make you most weary?

   Do those three activities qualify as "doing good"? Explain.

   What "harvest" do you hope to reap if you don't give up?

3. Read Hebrews 12:1. How has perseverance—sticking with it—paid off for you in the world of work or school? Give an example.

   If you applied that same relentlessness to the next year or two of mentoring your teen, how might it pay off?

4. Consider 1 Corinthians 15:58. When do you most feel like giving up on your teen?

   If being a spiritual mentor to your teen is "the work of the Lord," what can you expect if you resist the urge to give up?

5. Look up Matthew 28:20, Romans 8:37-39, and Hebrews 13:5. Which of these passages would be most encouraging to you when you're tempted to give up on your teen? Why?

strategies

Jim and Gina Michaels learned the hard way what it means to love relentlessly. When their daughter, Amanda, turned 17, it was as if someone "flipped a switch" to turn her from a sweet, good-natured, all-American girl next door into an angry, troubled teen. Almost overnight, she became sullen, brooding, and withdrawn. Everything about her body language screamed, "Stay away from me— I'm mad at the world!"

One night as Gina was putting away laundry in Amanda's dresser, she found a bag of marijuana. Disturbed and disappointed, Gina was not entirely surprised. That was, after all, just the latest in a series of unwise choices Amanda had made. When confronted by her parents, Amanda insisted that the bag of pot was a friend's and that she'd never even tried the stuff. When Jim asked if she were being completely honest, Amanda screamed, "I knew you wouldn't believe me! You've never trusted me! How can I tell you anything when you don't believe me?"

With each passing day, Jim and Gina felt their daughter becoming more distant and withdrawn. Seeking solutions, they met with their pastor and Amanda's youth pastor. Together, they devised a plan, including setting limits on Amanda's contact with friends who might be a negative influence and steering her toward positive experiences, such as church events and family outings. But underlying everything else was Jim and Gina's decision to be relentless in pursuit of their daughter.

"The number-one thing we decided was to persevere—to not surrender to our sense of hopelessness, to tell and show Amanda how much we cared, to do whatever it took to bring her around," Gina recalled. "We resolved to communicate in every way possible that we wouldn't abandon her or give up on her. She could try as hard as she wanted to push us away, but we would remain involved in her life no matter what."

As the months passed and Jim and Gina remained steadfast, they noticed that Amanda began to soften. Progress was slow, but her attitude gradually became more positive, and she showed fewer and fewer signs of rebelliousness. She reconnected with a couple of friends from her church youth group, she conversed more freely with her parents around the dinner table, and she showed renewed interest in her schoolwork.

Amanda and her parents saw a family counselor for several months to sort out what had happened and to rebuild their relationship. Toward the end of their therapy sessions, it was Amanda who pinpointed what had turned her around after nearly a year of rebellion:

"The thing that won me over was seeing my parents not give up on me. I pretended not to care when they said, 'We'll always be here for you,' but deep down, those words sank in. And they proved it through their actions, too. I also thought, *If they still love me after the terrible things I've done, maybe there's something to this Christianity stuff they've been talking about all these years.*"

Score another victory for relentless parenting.

The Seven Habits of Highly Relentless Parents

It's not just extreme cases like Amanda's that call for persistent parenting. Maintaining a relationship with any teen requires sticking with it. Here are seven practical ways to demonstrate that kind of relentlessness.

1. Pray, pray, pray. This habit is first on the list because that's where it belongs. The number-one strategy for guiding your child through the teen years is to surround him with prayer. Don't forget to include yourself in those prayers, too.

2. Choose to be involved. As reported in the book *Fantastic Families* (Howard Publishing, 1999), clinical researcher Dr. Nick Stinnett has conducted extensive studies on what makes strong families. After interviewing thousands of successful families, Stinnett and his colleagues identified six traits of close parent-child relationships. One characteristic is regular participation and involvement with each other.

Be involved in your teen's life whenever and however you can. Ask questions about her day. Play racquetball with him on the weekends. Go out to breakfast together. Be there for all the important events—and the seemingly unimportant ones.

Naturally, choosing to be involved in your child's life means taking a keen interest in his spiritual development. Provide every opportunity—whether at home, through church, or elsewhere—for your teenager's faith to grow.

3. Don't take no for an answer too easily. Of course you should respect your teen's boundaries, but some teenagers say "I don't want to talk about it" or "It's no big deal" because they're not sure their parents are really interested. Be persistent without being pushy. Assure your teen that you're genuinely interested and always available to listen.

4. *Emulate our heavenly Father's steadfast love.* God's love for each of His children is unchanging, enduring, and unwavering—regardless of how badly we blow it. Throughout the Old Testament, God declared and demonstrated His unyielding love for the Jews, His chosen people, even when they were rebellious and contemptuous toward Him:

> "Though the mountains be shaken and the hills be removed, yet my unfailing love for you will not be shaken." (Isaiah 54:10)

> "I have loved you with an everlasting love; I have drawn you with loving-kindness." (Jeremiah 31:3)

Let this kind of faithfulness be your model. Show and tell your teen often, "There's nothing you could do that would make me stop loving you."

5. *Renew your mercies every day.* Christians are fond of quoting the verse, "Through the Lord's mercies we are not consumed. . . . They are new every morning" (Lamentations 3:22-23, NKJV). As we savor the reassurance offered by this passage, let's extend this mercy to our teenagers. Every morning should bring a clean slate, a chance to start anew. If last night's argument was talked out and resolved, leave it behind. If your daughter apologized for the lie she told last week, believe that she's going to tell the truth today and tomorrow.

6. *Nurture yourself as you nurture your teen.* Green Bay Packers coach Vince Lombardi said, "Fatigue makes cowards of us all." Parents who are chronically drained of energy can offer little to their teenager. Guard your spiritual, emotional, and physical health. Recharge your batter-

ies: Get plenty of rest, set aside time for fun, exercise regularly, pray, and meditate on God's Word.

One of the best ways to nurture yourself is by developing a network of supportive friends—ideally other parents of teens—with whom you can share concerns, learn from one another's experiences, and pray for one another. If you aren't already part of a group like this or can't find one to join, take the initiative and start one in your church or community.

7. *Resolve to never, ever give up.* Decide now that you'll always be there for your teenager. No matter how angry, stressed-out, frustrated, disappointed, or exhausted you are, you'll be the best mom or dad you can be. Whether your teenager is gliding fluidly toward adulthood or stumbling badly, keep on cheering, encouraging, and applauding. Keep on offering your support and assistance. Keep on believing the best.

Keep on telling your son or daughter, "We're going to finish this race together!"

steps to take

1. Which of the following prayers do you most need to pray for your teen this week?
   a. That he or she won't give in to a particular temptation.
   b. That God will be more real to him or her.
   c. That he or she will be protected from a particular physical danger.
   d. That he or she will listen to you.
   e. Other _____

2. Which of these steps will you take to make sure you're involved in your teen's life?
   a. Go out to breakfast or lunch regularly
   b. Take up a shared activity like shooting baskets or going to concerts

c. Set a time each day to sit down and talk

d. Invite his or her friends over more often

e. Other _____

3. "Don't take no for an answer too easily." If the following exchanges occur between you and your teen, what will be your responses?

You: "What happened at school today?"

Your teen: "Nothing."

You: _____

You: "You look sad. Is something wrong?"

Your teen: "I don't want to talk about it."

You: _____

You: "I'd like to meet the kids you've been hanging around with."

Your teen: "They're too busy to come over."

You: _____

4. Even if you've told your teen, "There's nothing you could do that would make me stop loving you," there may be some things that would make it tough to keep loving him or her. Circle the items on this list that might fall into that category.

GETTING PREGNANT

GETTING A GIRL PREGNANT

WRECKING THE CAR

USING ILLEGAL DRUGS

GETTING DRUNK

FLUNKING A CLASS

BEING EXPELLED FROM SCHOOL

REJECTING YOUR FAITH

MOVING IN WITH A BOYFRIEND/GIRLFRIEND

LIVING A HOMOSEXUAL LIFESTYLE
BEING CONVICTED OF A CRIME
STEALING FROM YOU
USING PORNOGRAPHY
JOINING A GANG
JOINING A CULT
OTHER _____

What do you think would be God's attitude toward you if you did the things you just circled?

How can you emulate Him?

5. Imagine a chalkboard on which you've listed all the "bad attitudes" your teen has displayed even briefly in the last year. Cross out those that don't apply to your teen.

SARCASM
REBELLION
DISRESPECT
SELFISHNESS
DISOBEDIENCE
ARROGANCE
MALICE
INGRATITUDE
IRREVERENCE
LAZINESS
SUSPICION
DISHONESTY
GREED
SELF-PITY
IMPATIENCE
OTHER _____

Now cross out those that *do* apply—but that you're willing to forgive.

If there are any left, talk to God about the help you need to start with a "clean slate" in your relationship with your teen.

6. To maintain the energy you'll need to be relentless, which of the following steps will you take during the next month?
a. Improve your eating habits
b. Get more exercise
c. Get more sleep
d. Weed unnecessary commitments from your schedule
e. Join or form a network of supportive friends
f. Other _____

7. Are you willing to resolve never to give up on your teen? If so, fill in the blanks to complete the following pledge.

I, _____, hereby resolve to never, ever give up on my teen. Even if he or she _____, I will continue to _____. I will rely on God to give me strength in this effort by _____, and on the support of people by _____.

16

Learning to Let Go

startup

"If you love something, set it free."

"Just as a butterfly must emerge from its cocoon, so our children must be released to reach adulthood."

Birds. Butterflies. We've all heard those analogies about letting go of children so they can mature, spiritually and otherwise. It all sounds so simple—until we actually have to *do* it!

But that's part of a mentor's job.

Much as we might like to cage or cocoon our kids to protect them from the world (or themselves), the day will come when they're on their own. The time-honored "As long as you live under my roof, you'll follow my rules" will be an empty threat. We know, deep down, that's the way it should be. But it's not an easy prospect

to contemplate when you consider scenarios like
these:

- Your son goes off to college, where his philosophy
professor is a former preacher's kid who left the
faith and now takes delight in convincing his students to do the same.
- Your daughter starts her first job, where she meets a
charming, non-Christian guy who pressures her to
ditch church and spend cozy weekends with him at
his parents' beach cabin.
- Your son gets a roommate who keeps a marijuana
stash in the closet and is only too happy to share.
- Your daughter rents an apartment with a young
woman who is a very convincing spokesperson for
her faith—which happens to be Buddhism.

Chances are that you won't be there to "straighten
things out" when your newly liberated teen faces situations
like these. Your son or daughter will have life-shaping
choices to make—on his or her own.

survey

1. **When you think about "cutting the apron strings,"
what comes to mind?**
   a. The mom on *Leave It to Beaver*
   b. "Free at last, free at last . . ."
   c. Bungee jumping gone horribly awry
   d. Other _____

2. **Compared to other parents of teens, you're probably**
   a. A bit overprotective
   b. A bit underprotective
   c. A bit tired of comparing yourself to other parents of
   teens
   d. Other _____

3. **When did you begin preparing your child for the day when he'll be on his own?**
   a. Just before conception
   b. When he started kindergarten
   c. What do you mean, "On his own"?
   d. Other _____

4. **You'll know your child "owns his faith" when he**
   a. Studies Scripture by himself
   b. Stops asking whether Adam had a belly button
   c. Tries to sell it to you
   d. Other _____

5. **Spiritually speaking, when did your parents decide you were on your own?**
   a. When you went on the church-building trip to Latin America
   b. After the incident with the firecrackers and the jar of peanut butter
   c. What do you mean, "On my own"?
   d. Other _____

scripture

1. Read Luke 2:39-52. What evidence do you see here that Jesus was ready to be "on His own" spiritually?

   Do you think Joseph and Mary were ready to let Him go? Why or why not?

   How are Jesus' attitude and behavior here like those of your teen? How are they different?

If you'd been in the sandals of Joseph or Mary, would you have reacted to this incident by (a) grounding Jesus, (b) warning Him not to do it again, (c) letting Him stay in Jerusalem, or (d) something else? Why?

2. Examine 2 Kings 2:8-15. Let's say you ask your teen, "Tell me, what can I do for you—spiritually speaking— before I am taken from you?" What might be your teen's reply? What kind of preparation do you think he or she might want most?

strategies

How can you prepare your child for the not-too-distant future?

Here are three ways to go about it—three "prep points" that can get teens ready to spread their wings without going down in flames:

Prep Point 1: Make Sure Your Teen Owns His Faith

Look for these five signs that your adolescent is beginning to own his faith:

1. He wants to discover more about God and what it means to belong to Him. The evidence: an interest in Bible reading, prayer, and asking questions.

2. She doesn't have to be nagged into being involved with other Christian teens.

3. Given time, he can explain *in his own words* how he became a Christian and why he wants to live like one.

4. She shows an interest in what God might want as she plans for the future.

5. His views about how biblical principles should be

applied sometimes differ from your own, or they are at least expressed in different ways.

That last point is a tough one. As parents, we need to distinguish between faith essentials and parental tastes—being sure to pass along the former and be flexible with the latter.

Where should you draw that line with your teen? Here are five questions to ask yourself when you need to decide:

1. *Is my child's eternal destiny at stake here?* It's easy to forget, but the gospel boils down to a pretty simple statement: "Believe in the Lord Jesus, and you will be saved" (Acts 16:31).

2. *Am I upset because my teen is rejecting the Bible or because I feel rejected?* Is your child really discounting Scripture or just interpreting it in a way that differs from your own?

3. *Is this issue addressed in historic statements of what's essential in the Christian faith?* If not, it may be a matter of preference.

4. *Is this worth risking our relationship?* If the issue doesn't threaten your teen's safety, consider avoiding ultimatums in order to continue having a long-term influence.

5. *Do I need to leave this in God's hands?* Keep loving and praying for your teen. Like many adolescents, she may be tearing her faith apart—in order to put it back together again in a form she can truly own.

Prep Point 2: Give Kids Increasing Freedom to Make Choices

The second thing we can do to ready kids for independence is to let them make as many decisions as possible. It's great to help teens turn their beliefs into convictions, but we must go a step further and let them start *applying* those convictions, too.

"But it's risky to let kids make choices," you might say.

And you'd be right. Our teens will never truly grow up unless we take those risks, however. The key is to minimize them.

How? Dean Merrill (*Focus on the Family* magazine, October 1996) recommends finding "safe settings" in which to use what he calls the Two Magic Words of Parenting: "You decide."

Call it *empowerment* if you like. That's the $50 word for letting your kids make safe but significant choices. If we want our teens to make sound decisions when they're out of the nest, they need to hear us say "You decide" as often as possible—while they're still under our wings.

Prep Point 3: Give Kids Increasing Responsibility

The third way to prepare teens for independence is to hand them more responsibility. This means taking off the spiritual training wheels and letting kids pedal the straight and narrow for themselves—even if the ride is a bit wobbly.

Joe White, in *FaithTraining* (Focus on the Family, 1994), suggests that kids take on the following responsibilities at approximately the following ages:

Age 12—Regular youth group attendance
Age 13.5—Daily quiet times
Age 14—Small, peer-group Bible study
Age 15—Lifestyle witnessing to friends
Age 17—Intellectual preparation (apologetics, etc.) for college
Age 18—Summer missionary trip or serving/giving job

No two children are alike, of course; all mature at different rates. Some young people struggle with certain tasks because of personality, disability, or emotional trauma and should not be expected to achieve as others can.

Here are five areas in which most teens can begin to take responsibility:

1. *Their relationship with God.* When children are young, some parents try to act as "middle men" in their little ones' link with the Lord. By adolescence, if not long before, kids need to understand that their connection with God is direct.

2. *Spiritual disciplines.* Prayer, Bible reading and memorization, giving to the Lord's work—all are activities most teens can handle.

3. *Church involvement.* Some teens can't stand to miss a single youth-group meeting, Bible study, or retreat. Others would rather be skinned alive than darken a church door. You may want to set a minimum requirement for church attendance, but give your teen options beyond that point. For instance, let him choose to attend Sunday school *or* a small discipleship group.

4. *Living their faith.* When our children are small, we may try to help them resist temptation by hiding the cookie jar. But we won't be able to do that when our teens leave the nest. Adolescents need to know that saying no to wrong and yes to right is up to them.

5. *Finding answers to their questions.* It feels good to be the "fount of wisdom" when our pre-teens come to us, wide-eyed and trusting, with their queries. In adolescence, however, those wide eyes tend to narrow considerably. Fortunately, teens need to practice answer-hunting anyway. Instead of playing oracle, point your child toward helpful books, pamphlets, and Web sites.

Sending Strong Kids to College
Many adolescents seize graduation as a chance to break with childhood—and religious activities are often the first to go.

Your own college-bound teen's story will be unique. But it's more likely to end happily if you get ready for college in the following ways:

1. *Let your teen know that your family is rooting for her.*

Things can get lonely when you're a student. Communicate your family's continuing solidarity through e-mail, phone calls, and notes.

2. *Be the kind of parent your child can run to.* Starting now, make it clear that doubts and questions won't alienate you.

3. *Prepare for the debate.* Your teen's faith will be challenged during the next few years—guaranteed. The challenges may be issued by an agnostic professor, a skeptical co-worker, or the disappointment of a broken romance. Just as political candidates stage "dry runs" with stand-in opponents to get ready for debates, you can bring up tough questions in advance and seek answers together.

4. *Make the church hunt as easy as possible.* Don't try to pick your teen's college-town church for her, but make the search simpler. Look together at Yellow Pages and newspaper church listings for the area. If possible, visit one or more congregations near the campus.

5. *Pray.* You'll probably be doing a lot of this when your teen is off on his own. You may as well start now!

steps to take

1. Does your teen own his faith? On a scale of 1 to 10 (1 being weakly, 10 being strongly), circle a number to show how well he's doing in each of the following areas:

   He wants to discover more about God and what it means to belong to Him.
   1 2 3 4 5 6 7 8 9 10

   She doesn't have to be nagged into being involved with other Christian teens.
   1 2 3 4 5 6 7 8 9 10

Given time, he can explain in his own words how he became a Christian and why he wants to live like one.
1 2 3 4 5 6 7 8 9 10

She shows an interest in what God might want as she plans for the future.
1 2 3 4 5 6 7 8 9 10

His views about how biblical principles should be applied sometimes differ from your own, or they're at least expressed in different ways.
1 2 3 4 5 6 7 8 9 10

2. On which of the following issues do you and your teen disagree?
   a. Creation and evolution
   b. Dating non-Christians
   c. The need to attend church
   d. Appropriate music
   e. Other _____

   Regarding one of those areas of disagreement, answer the following:

   Is your child's eternal destiny at stake here?

   Is your child really ignoring the Bible or just interpreting it in a way that differs from your own?

   Is this issue addressed in historic statements of what's essential in the Christian faith, or is it a matter of preference?

Is it worth risking your relationship over?

Do you need to leave this in God's hands? If not, what specific action do you need to take this week?

3. Which of the following choices would you be willing to let your teen make during the next month?
   a. Whether to brush his teeth
   b. Whether to drink alcohol
   c. Whether to go to a dance
   d. Whether to be home-schooled
   e. Whether to join the military
   f. Whether to attend church
   g. Whether to stay up past 10 P.M. on school nights
   h. Whether to watch reruns of *Will & Grace*

4. How does your teen's progress compare with the timetable suggested by Joe White? After each goal, circle the response that most closely matches yours.
   Age 12—Regular youth group attendance
   a. Your teen met this goal
   b. Your teen met this goal later
   c. Your teen hasn't met this goal
   d. Your teen doesn't need to meet this goal
   e. You and your teen have work to do in this area

   Age 13.5—Daily quiet times
   a. Your teen met this goal
   b. Your teen met this goal later
   c. Your teen hasn't met this goal
   d. Your teen doesn't need to meet this goal
   e. You and your teen have work to do in this area

Age 14—Small, peer-group Bible study
a. Your teen met this goal
b. Your teen met this goal later
c. Your teen hasn't met this goal
d. Your teen doesn't need to meet this goal
e. You and your teen have work to do in this area

Age 15—Lifestyle witnessing to friends
a. Your teen met this goal
b. Your teen met this goal later
c. Your teen hasn't met this goal
d. Your teen doesn't need to meet this goal
e. You and your teen have work to do in this area

Age 17—Intellectual preparation (apologetics, etc.) for college
a. Your teen met this goal
b. Your teen met this goal later
c. Your teen hasn't met this goal
d. Your teen doesn't need to meet this goal
e. You and your teen have work to do in this area

Age 18—Summer missionary trip or serving/giving job
a. Your teen met this goal
b. Your teen met this goal later
c. Your teen hasn't met this goal
d. Your teen doesn't need to meet this goal
e. You and your teen have work to do in this area

5. What will you do this week to prepare your teen for college or career independence? From the following list, choose just one step you'll actually take.

___ Write a note letting him know your family is rooting for him

___ Tell him about doubts you had concerning Christianity when you were a teen, and let him know that such questions won't alienate you

___ Give him a book or video that makes a good case for the reliability of the Bible

___ Role play a conversation in which he explains his faith to a professor, fellow student, or co-worker

___ Look together at Yellow Pages or newspaper church listings for the area in which he plans to live

___ Other _____

Leader's Guide

This leader's guide is designed to help you turn the rest of the book into a lively group experience in which parents learn from and support each other.

Before each meeting, have group members read and complete the corresponding chapter. You'll want to read and complete the chapter, too—and review the plan for that session.

The Session Plan

We're assuming you have about 45-60 minutes to spend on each meeting. Ideally, your session time should be used for discussing and applying what group members have already learned by "doing the homework" in advance. Your meeting might look something like this:

1. *Optional Opener* (5 minutes). If your group is into fun and you have time, start with this activity.

2. *Startup* (5 minutes). Ask a couple of volunteers to share their reactions to the chapter introduction.

3. *Survey* (5 minutes). Let a few people explain one or two of their picks in this multiple-choice section.

4. *Scripture* (5-10 minutes). Volunteers can tell which question and answer were most meaningful to them.

5. *Strategies* (10-15 minutes). Discuss key points from the article that's at the heart of the chapter.

6. *Steps to Take* (15-20 minutes). Give group members time to share their responses and to pray for the success of each other's plans.

If participants won't do the homework, you'll need to change your approach. Your meeting might go as follows:

1. *Optional Opener* (5 minutes). Have fun with this if you've got the time.

2. *Scripture* (10-15 minutes). Together or in smaller groups, read the Bible passages and discuss the questions.

3. *Strategies* (10-15 minutes). Summarize the article or have participants take turns reading it aloud. Let volunteers respond to the advice.

4. *Steps to Take* (20-25 minutes). Work through this application section together, individually, or in teams; close by letting volunteers share some of their answers and plans.

Whichever approach you take, encourage group members to prepare for your times together. They'll get more from the course if they do.

Tips for Success
Want to lead your group with maximum confidence? Here are some suggestions.

- If your group is like most, you often run out of time before you run out of discussion questions and activities. What to do? Simply choose the exercises and questions you think will be most meaningful to your group and concentrate on those. Try starting with the bare essentials—discussing the "Strategies" section and applying the principles through the final "Steps to Take" activities. Add more as your schedule allows.
- Invite discussion, but don't be surprised if some group members are reluctant to share personal information. It's hard to admit one's mistakes as a parent—or to talk about painful childhood experiences. If people want to reflect silently on a probing question, encourage them to do so.
- It's a good idea to have a few extra copies of the book on hand, so that visitors (and those who forgot their books) can take part.
- If you don't have an answer to every parenting question, join the club! It's okay to say, "I don't know." Ask group members to share wisdom from their experience. Refer people to the *Parents' Guide to the Spiritual Mentoring of Teens* (Focus on the Family/Tyndale, 2001), on which this book is based. Encourage those who face especially difficult parenting situations to consult your pastor or a counselor.
- Have a good time! Parenting may be serious business, but most of your group members probably would appreciate a light touch as they learn. Let your group be a place where parents can enjoy each other and gain perspective on their teen mentoring challenges.
- Pray. Pray for your group members during the week. Urge them to pray for each other. Ask God to help each person become the loving, effective parent he or she was meant to be.

Ready to have a lasting, positive impact on the parents and teens represented in your group? May God bless you as you lead!

PART 1: BECOMING YOUR TEEN'S SPIRITUAL COACH

Session 1
What Mentors Are Meant For

1. *Optional Opener*
If time allows and your group is open to having a little fun, try the following activity. Bring 30 sheets of paper.

Form three teams. Team 1 chooses its most experienced maker of paper airplanes to be its "mentor"; Team 2 does the same. But Team 3 picks its *least* experienced plane maker.

Team 1 must take instructions from its mentor as it tries to make 10 flyable planes. Team 3 does the same. Team 2 can only watch as its mentor makes all the planes himself or herself. Only mentors are allowed to speak.

When two minutes are up, see which team has the most airworthy planes. Then ask:

Which mentor do you think taught his or her team the most? Why?

What does this tell you about mentoring?

2. *Startup*
To encourage brief discussion of the chapter introduction, ask:

When it comes to guiding their teenagers spiritually, do you think most parents are like coaches, or are they still trying to play the game for their kids? Or are they ignoring the issue completely?

If group members haven't read the "Startup" and "Survey" sections, don't take the time to do so now. Instead, go directly to the "Scripture" section.

3. *Survey*
If group members have completed this multiple-choice feature on their own, they may have a few answers—humorous or serious—to share. Let a few volunteers do so. Then ask:

What do you *really* hope will be different in your house as a result of this course?

4. Scripture

If your group is large, form pairs or teams to discuss the answers participants came up with during the week. Then regather the whole group and let spokespersons summarize the teams' findings. For groups who haven't done the homework, allow more time to read and discuss the Bible passages in the book.

Whether or not people have prepared, you might find it useful to ask these follow-up questions:

King Solomon is known as the wisest man in the world. Do you suppose his son saw him that way? Why or why not?

When it came to spiritual mentoring, what resources did Solomon have available to him that you don't have? How about vice versa?

5. Strategies

Groups who haven't read the advice article will need time to become familiar with its content. You can summarize it, read it aloud, let volunteers take turns reading it, or have everyone read it silently.

Once people are up to speed, try asking questions like these:

Do you welcome the change from governor to mentor, or dread it? Why?

Is your teen more like Brianna or Derek? How should that affect the way you mentor him or her?

What fictional mentor are you most like? Which one would you *like* to resemble? Why?

6. Steps to Take

To make the application as personal as possible, and to give everyone a chance to talk, form pairs or teams if your group has more than four members. If participants have worked through this section on their own, spend as much time as you can letting them share their responses. Otherwise, have people work through selected questions (we'd suggest numbers 1, 3, and 4) now.

If time allows, follow up with questions like these:

Do you feel ready to follow through on any of the suggestions in this chapter?

If so, which one needs to be your top priority?

If not, what would help you feel more ready?

To close, encourage pairs or teams to pray for the success of group members' plans. If possible, be available after the meeting to hear participants' concerns, and to refer to a pastor or counselor any who are seriously struggling with their teens.

Session 2
You Can Do It!

1. Optional Opener

If time allows and your group is open to having a little fun, try the following activity.

Form two teams. Tell them they're going to compete in performing a short list of very easy tasks. If possible, have them stand as they try to follow these instructions. Read the list quickly, without pausing between items.

- Rub your stomach and pat your head.
- Pat your stomach and rub your head.
- Rub your elbow, pat your knee, and recite the first 12 letters of the alphabet.
- Pat yourself on the back, rub the sleep out of your eyes, and walk like an Egyptian.
- Toe the line, make the grade, get on the stick, shape up, and pass muster.

Chances are that neither team will be able to follow the instructions completely, especially the last set. After thanking those who tried, ask:

Which instruction was hardest to follow? Why?

Were all my directions clear? Was I expecting you to do too much?

When I talk about being a spiritual mentor to your teen, does it sound anything like my instructions in this exercise? If so, how?

2. Startup

To encourage brief discussion of the chapter introduction, ask:

Which of these doubts do you relate to most? Why?

If group members haven't read the "Startup" and "Survey" sections, don't take the time to do so now. Instead, go directly to the "Scripture" section.

3. Survey

If group members have completed this multiple-choice feature on their own, they may have a few answers—humorous or serious—to share. Let a few volunteers do so. Then ask:

When you think about the fact that your teen's future is on the line, does that make spiritual mentoring sound more scary, less scary, or just more necessary? Why?

4. Scripture

If your group is large, form pairs or teams to discuss the answers participants came up with during the week. Then regather the whole group and let spokespersons summarize the teams' findings. For groups who haven't done the homework, allow more time to read and discuss the Bible passages in the book.

Follow up the discussion by having people choose to memorize either 2 Corinthians 12:9-10 or Isaiah 40:30-31 as a way to encourage themselves this week. If time allows, let them try to learn one of those passages now.

5. Strategies

Groups who haven't read the advice article will need time to become familiar with its content. You can summarize it, read it aloud, let volunteers take turns reading it, or have everyone read it silently.

Once people are up to speed, try asking questions like these:

Which of the six concerns do you think is most common among parents of teens?

Which of the six do you think is hardest to overcome?

Which do you think your *teen* would identify as a problem in your home?

Do you believe God really wants you to take these concerns to Him? Why or why not?

6. Steps to Take

In case group members don't want to reveal the areas in which they feel inadequate, let them work individually or as couples on the exercises that apply. Give them a chance to share results with the group, but don't press for responses. That's also true if participants have already completed this section.

Spend the rest of the session praying for each other. Break the group into pairs or trios and ask them to pray along these lines:

- That God will help each parent set realistic goals and make the most of the time left with his or her teen.
- That parents who are "going it alone" will find other mentors to supplement their efforts.
- That damaged parent-teen relationships would be healed.
- That those who weren't mentored well themselves would be able to forgive those who failed them and move ahead.
- That parents who are tempted to give up will get a "second wind."

- That parents would have the courage to be honest—and imperfect—role models for their teens.

Session 3
The Goal of Spiritual Training

1. Optional Opener
If time allows and your group is open to having a little fun, play Pin the Tail on the Target. Bring a Post-it note, tape, and a target you've drawn on a piece of heavy paper or poster board.

Hold up the target. Ask a volunteer if he thinks he can stick the Post-it note on the bull's-eye. Explain that unlike Pin the Tail on the Donkey, this game is played without a blindfold.

Tape the target to the wall—but facing the wall. Your volunteer, who probably will be surprised by this development, must try to put the "sticky note" where the bull's-eye would be without being able to see it.

Whether the volunteer succeeds or not, congratulate him. Then discuss the difficulty of hitting a target when you can't see it. Ask:

Have you ever tried to reach a goal when you weren't sure what or where it was? What happened?

When it comes to spiritually training your teen, how do you know whether you're hitting the target?

Do you think most parents have goals for their teenagers' spiritual growth? Why or why not?

2. Startup
To encourage brief discussion of the chapter introduction, ask:

Does this graduation scenario make you nervous, eager, or something else? Why?

If group members haven't read the "Startup" and "Survey" sections, don't take the time to do so now. Instead, go directly to the "Scripture" section.

3. Survey
If group members have completed this multiple-choice feature on their own, they may have a few answers—humorous or serious—to share. Let a few volunteers do so. Then ask:

Have you ever set a goal for your child's spiritual growth? If so, what happened? If not, why not?

4. Scripture

If your group is large, form pairs or teams to discuss the answers participants came up with during the week. Then regather the whole group and let spokespersons summarize the teams' findings. For groups who haven't done the homework, allow more time to read and discuss the Bible passages in the book.

Whether or not people have prepared, you might find it useful to ask these follow-up questions:

How many goals for spiritual training do you suppose the Bible contains?

If you could boil all those goals down to half a dozen or so, what might they be?

5. Strategies

Groups who haven't read the advice article will need time to become familiar with its content. You can summarize it, read it aloud, let volunteers take turns reading it, or have everyone read it silently.

Once people are up to speed, try asking questions like these:

Is there any way to prioritize these goals? Do some need to be accomplished before others? Explain.

Are there any goals you'd add to this list? If so, what are they? If not, why not? Do these targets apply to Christians of any age? Why or why not?

6. Steps to Take

To make the application as personal as possible, and to give everyone a chance to talk, form pairs or teams if your group has more than four members. If participants have worked through this section on their own, spend as much time as you can letting them share their responses. If people are reluctant to talk about areas in which their teens are struggling, let them concentrate on setting measurable goals to work toward. If participants haven't done the homework, have them work through selected questions (we'd suggest numbers 1, 2, and 4) individually or as couples.

If time allows, follow up with questions like these:

What's one area in which your child already has grown spiritually, even a little?

How could that fact encourage you this week?

Read Proverbs 21:31. How could this verse help you as you work toward your goals?

To close, encourage pairs or teams to pray for the success of group members' plans. If possible, be available after the meeting to hear participants' concerns, and to refer to a pastor or counselor any who need more help.

Session 4
Helping Your Teen to Own His Faith

1. Optional Opener
Bring something that means a lot to you or your family—but that won't mean much to others. This might be a video or photo album of a family vacation or a relative's wedding, a collection of postcards from friends, or Christmas cards you've received. Subject the group to watching the video or looking at the cards or letters, being sure to declare how fascinating the whole thing is.

Then say:

Be honest. On a scale of 1 to 10 (10 highest), how interesting was this to you?

Why was this less fascinating to you than it was to me?

Generally speaking, do things mean less when they aren't yours? Why?

If your teen's faith isn't really her own, what might the consequences be?

2. Startup
To encourage brief discussion of the chapter introduction, ask:

Where did things start to go wrong for Marilyn?

If you were Marilyn's mother, what might you wish you'd done differently?

If group members haven't read the "Startup" and "Survey" sections, don't take the time to do so now. Instead, go directly to the "Scripture" section.

3. Survey
If group members have completed this multiple-choice feature on their own, they may have a few answers—humorous or serious—to share. Let a few volunteers do so. Then ask:

Which do you think is harder to talk with a teenager about—the "facts of life" or the state of his or her faith? Why?

If you had to bring up the subject of whether your teen is really a believer, how would you do it?

4. Scripture
If your group is large, form pairs or teams to discuss the answers participants came up with during the week. Then regather the whole group and let spokespersons summarize the teams' findings. For groups who haven't done the homework, allow more time to read and discuss the Bible passages in the book.

Do you think people are more likely to "depart" from the faith when they're pre-teens, teens, young adults, middle-aged, or elderly? Why?

Taken together, do these Scriptures encourage you to be optimistic or pessimistic about your teen's spiritual future? Why?

5. Strategies
Groups who haven't read the advice article will need time to become familiar with its content. You can summarize it, read it aloud, let volunteers take turns reading it, or have everyone read it silently.

Once people are up to speed, try asking questions like these:

How might your teenager react to the suggestions in this article?

When you were your teen's age, did people think you were a Christian? Why or why not? Were they right?

When you were your teen's age, had you formed many of your own convictions? If so, how did that happen?

Which part of this article is of the most interest to you right now? Why?

6. Steps to Take
Form pairs or teams if your group has more than four members. If participants have worked through this section on their own, spend as much time as you can letting them share their responses. Group members who aren't comfortable revealing doubts about their teens' spiritual state may want to concentrate on questions 1, 6, and 7. If participants haven't done the homework, have them work through selected questions (we'd suggest numbers 1, 4, and 6) individually or as couples.

If time allows, follow up with questions like these:

When it comes to leading a teenager to Christ, how much depends on the parent, how much depends on the teen, and how much depends on God?

When it comes to forming convictions, how much depends on the parent, how much depends on the teen, and how much depends on God?

What do you need to depend on God for this week?

To close, encourage pairs or teams to pray for each other, and for their teenagers.

PART 2: BUILDING A GREAT RELATIONSHIP WITH YOUR TEEN

Session 5
The Ties That Bond

1. *Optional Opener*

If time allows and your group is open to having a little fun, try the following activity.

Bring as many unattractive neckties as you can find (check secondhand stores, rummage sales, and closet floors for likely candidates). Let people pick the ones they think are worst, and stage an "Ugly Tie Contest." Group members should take turns modeling the ties, followed by a vote to choose the most obnoxious.

Then say:

In this course we're going to talk about the "ties" that bind parents and teens. Sometimes those ties can get pretty ugly.

What kinds of problems can make a parent-teen tie turn ugly?

How does an "ugly tie" between you and your teen affect your ability to be his or her spiritual mentor?

2. *Startup*

To encourage brief discussion of the chapter introduction, ask:

How might this story have turned out differently if Janna's mom had been having a bad day? What if she were late for an appointment?

Does anything about this mom's response surprise you? If so, what might that say about the way parents usually respond to their teenagers?

If group members haven't read the "Startup" and "Survey" sections, don't take the time to do so now. Instead, go directly to the "Scripture" section.

3. *Survey*

If group members have completed this multiple-choice feature on their own, they may have a few answers—humorous or serious—to share. Let a few volunteers do so. Then call attention to number four. Ask:

Have you ever heard the saying, "Rules without relationship lead to rebellion"? What do you think it means?

4. Scripture

If your group is large, form pairs or teams to discuss the answers participants came up with during the week. Then regather the whole group and let spokespersons summarize the teams' findings. For groups who haven't done the homework, allow more time to read and discuss the Bible passages in the book.

Whether or not people have prepared, you might find it useful to ask these follow-up questions:

Do you have to get all these relationship factors right before you can be your teen's spiritual mentor? If not, which ones do you think are most important?

How can you have a good relationship with your teen despite flaws and mistakes? What qualities help the "tie" to survive in spite of imperfections?

5. Strategies

Groups who haven't read the advice article will need time to become familiar with its content. You can summarize it, read it aloud, let volunteers take turns reading it, or have everyone read it silently.

Once people are up to speed, try asking questions like these:

Is this list of relationship builders a little overwhelming? Why or why not? Which of these relationship builders do you think your teen would most like to see more of?

Which relationship *buster* might your teen want you to work on first?

What's one thing you'd like to see your *teen* do to build your relationship?

6. Steps to Take

To make the application as personal as possible, and to give everyone a chance to talk, form pairs or teams if your group has more than four members. If participants have worked through this section on their own, spend as much time as you can letting them share their responses. Otherwise, have people work through selected questions (we'd suggest numbers 1, 2, 5, and 6) now.

If time allows, follow up with questions like these:

What idea from this session leaves you saying, "I'm not sure I agree with that"?

What idea from this session leaves you saying, "I need to try that this week"?

What idea from this session leaves you saying, "I need more time to think about that"?

To close, encourage pairs or teams to pray for the success of group members' plans.

Session 6
Learning to Be a Great Communicator

1. Optional Opener
Before the session, write each of the following four sets of instructions on a separate index card.

1. *Parent:* You're finally getting around to addressing an embarrassing topic. *Teen:* You're bored with what your parent is saying, and can barely wait for the conversation to end.

2. *Parent:* You're angry with your teen and feel he or she has betrayed your trust. *Teen:* You feel unfairly accused by your parent.

3. *Parent:* You feel guilty about an argument you had with your teen last night. *Teen:* You're enjoying seeing your parent squirm.

4. *Parent:* You're excited about something that happened to you and want to tell the whole story. *Teen:* You had a terrible day at school and think everyone should know it instinctively.

Set up two chairs in the front of the room. When the meeting starts, get volunteers to sit on the chairs and play the roles of the parents and teens. Each pair should act out the situation on its index card using only body language and pantomime—no words. See whether the rest of the group can guess the emotions and attitudes the role-players are communicating.

Then ask:

In a real-life conversation, are you good at deciphering your teen's body language?

What percentage of communication do you think depends on words, and what percentage on body language and gestures?

How do our communication skills shape our relationships with our teens?

2. Startup
To encourage brief discussion of the chapter introduction, ask:

Have you ever had a conversation like this? Do you know a "cure" for it? Is the idea of the sullen, silent teen just a stereotype, or does it have its basis in reality? What are some other common communication barriers between parents and teens?

If group members haven't read the "Startup" and "Survey" sections, don't take the time to do so now. Instead, go directly to the "Scripture" section.

3. Survey

If group members have completed this multiple-choice feature on their own, they may have a few answers—humorous or serious—to share. Let a few volunteers do so. Then ask:

How are communication problems between parents and teens usually depicted in TV sitcoms? In dramas?

When does parent-teen miscommunication stop being funny and start having serious consequences?

4. Scripture

If your group is large, form pairs or teams to discuss the answers participants came up with during the week. Then regather the whole group and let spokespersons summarize the teams' findings. For groups who haven't done the homework, allow more time to read and discuss the Bible passages in the book.

Follow up the discussion by asking questions like these:

Which one of these Scriptures, if you applied it, might make the biggest difference in the way you communicate with your teenager?

Could it help if you memorized that passage and reminded yourself of it this week? At what times would you most need to remember it?

5. Strategies

Groups who haven't read the advice article will need time to become familiar with its content. You can summarize it, read it aloud, let volunteers take turns reading it, or have everyone read it silently.

Once people are up to speed, try asking questions like these:

Based on this article, how could you improve the following approaches to parent-teen communication?

- Trying to start a conversation by saying, "We never talk anymore."
- In the middle of dinner, bringing up the subject of last night's broken curfew.

- During an argument about wasting money, reminding your teen of the time he ran out of gas while driving on the freeway.
- Saying, "If I'm a dork, you're dorkier!"

6. Steps to Take

To make the application as personal as possible, and to give everyone a chance to talk, form pairs or teams if your group has more than four members. If participants have worked through this section on their own, spend as much time as you can letting them share their responses. Otherwise, have people concentrate on question 1 now.

If time allows, follow up with questions like these:

Which do you want to work on more—the quantity of communication with your teen, the quality, or both?

How will you be able to tell when you and your teen are communicating well?

A TV commercial for wireless communication once asked the question, "Can you hear me now?" If you asked your teen that, what might he or she reply?

If your teen asked you that question, what would you say? Why?

To close, encourage pairs or teams to pray for each other's efforts to improve communication with their teens.

Session 7
Giving Grace

1. Optional Opener

Bring several slices of cold, burnt toast that you've cut into little squares. Serve these on a platter, acting as if they're scrumptious party treats.

When the group is less than enthusiastic, say:

These refreshments didn't turn out quite the way I'd hoped. But don't worry—I'll do better next time. As a matter of fact, I'd like to cater your next big social event. How many of you would let me do that?

Give people a chance to respond. You probably won't get a lot of takers.

Are you saying you won't give me a second chance?

After volunteers reply, continue:

What if I were your teenager? Would you give me a second chance then?

Listen to people's answers.

How do you decide when to give your teen a second chance?

After volunteers respond, explain:

In this session we'll talk about how much our teenagers need second chances—in other words, how they need grace. And we'll explore how giving grace can pave the way for spiritual growth.

2. Startup

To encourage brief discussion of the chapter introduction, ask:

Do you think more parents make mental "highlights" tapes or "blooper" tapes of their teens' behavior? Why?

Which is harder—forgiving your teen's mistakes, or forgetting them? Why?

If group members haven't read the "Startup" and "Survey" sections, don't take the time to do so now. Instead, go directly to the "Scripture" section.

3. Survey

If group members have completed this multiple-choice feature on their own, they may have a few answers—humorous or serious—to share. Let a few volunteers do so. Then ask:

How do you think your teenager would define "grace"?

Does your family seem to need more second chances than most? Explain.

4. Scripture

If your group is large, form pairs or teams to discuss the answers participants came up with during the week. Then regather the whole group and let spokespersons summarize the teams' findings. For groups who haven't done the homework, allow more time to read and discuss the Bible passages in the book.

Whether or not people have prepared, you might find it useful to ask these follow-up questions:

With whom do you identify most in these Bible passages? The king, the servant, the fellow-servant, or Peter? Why?

With whom do you think your teen would most identify?

5. Strategies

Groups who haven't read the advice article will need time to become familiar with its content. If you think participants would be embarrassed by reading aloud the

"Spiritual Growth and Failure" section, which mentions masturbation as an example of guilt-causing teen behavior, let people read the article silently or summarize the key points yourself.

Once people are up to speed, try asking questions like these:

What are some other behaviors that might cause a young person to feel like a failure and want to avoid getting closer to God?

If your teen struggled with an eating disorder like anorexia and felt like a failure as a result, what kind of conversation could you have with her that offered grace? What if the problem were an addiction to alcohol?

What do you think is the most important thing to remember about the story of Rob? Why?

6. Steps to Take

To make the application as personal as possible, and to give everyone a chance to talk, form pairs or teams if your group has more than four members. If participants have worked through this section on their own, spend as much time as you can letting them share their responses. Some may be reluctant to do so with questions 2, 3, and 6, which deal with their teens' personal struggles; if so, have them concentrate on the other questions. If people haven't prepared, have them work through selected exercises (we'd suggest numbers 1, 5, and 7) now.

If time allows, follow up by asking this:

What's one new idea you're thinking about as a result of this discussion?

To close, have pairs or teams pray for each other's efforts to show grace to their teens.

Session 8
Becoming Your Teen's Biggest Fan

1. Optional Opener

Try the following if you have time. Form two or more teams of "cheerleaders." Assign each team to come up with a cheer that celebrates an everyday victory a teen might experience—like getting the lawn mowed or waking up without an acne attack. Here's an example:

"No one's as smart as Elizabeth is!

Got 90 percent on the algebra quiz!
She aced those equations as quick as could be—
If she'll just get that scholarship, college is free! Yay!"
Here's another example:
"Ricky, Ricky, he's no slouch,
Found the TV remote down under the couch!
Now we can all stare at the idiot box—
It's better than housework and picking up socks! Go, Ricky!"
Let teams perform their cheers for the whole group. If you like, vote to pick the best. Then ask:

Who are the cheerleaders in your teen's life?

Which of your teen's achievements tend to get the most praise?

How could becoming your teen's biggest fan affect your relationship?

2. Startup

To encourage brief discussion of the chapter introduction, ask:

Do you think most parents "cheer" when their teens show signs of spiritual growth? Why or why not?

What might cause a parent *not* to cheer a teen's accomplishments?

If group members haven't read the "Startup" and "Survey" sections, don't take the time to do so now. Instead, go directly to the "Scripture" section.

3. Survey

If group members have completed this multiple-choice feature on their own, they may have a few answers—humorous or serious—to share. Let a few volunteers do so. Then ask:

When you affirm your teen, how does he or she usually respond? Does that encourage you to do this more often or less often?

4. Scripture

If your group is large, form pairs or teams to discuss the answers participants came up with during the week. Then regather the whole group and let spokespersons summarize the teams' findings. For groups who haven't done the homework, allow more time to read and discuss the Bible passages in the book.

Whether or not people have prepared, you might find it useful to ask these follow-up questions:

Does your teen receive encouragement at church? If so, what kind? If not, why not?

Do these passages apply at home as much as they do in the church body? Why or why not?

5. Strategies

Groups who haven't read the advice article will need time to become familiar with its content. You can summarize it, read it aloud, let volunteers take turns reading it, or have everyone read it silently.

Once people are up to speed, try asking questions like these:

What do you think would happen if you tried the following suggestions from the article?

- Writing your teen's upcoming events on a calendar to make sure you know which ones to attend.
- Sneaking an encouraging card into your teen's backpack.
- Writing four good things about your teen in a journal each day.
- Making five positive comments about your teen for every negative one you make.
- Letting your teen be the navigator on your next family vacation.
- Asking your teen what she thinks you should do with a tax refund.

6. Steps to Take

To make the application as personal as possible, and to give everyone a chance to talk, form pairs or teams if your group has more than four members. If participants have worked through this section on their own, spend as much time as you can letting them share their responses. Otherwise, have people work through any three of the questions now.

If possible, follow up with questions like these:

What will you do if your teen doesn't respond immediately or positively to your cheerleading?

If you're doing this without a spouse's help, how can the rest of us make it easier?

To close, ask each group member to "cheer on" the person sitting at his or her right—saying something encouraging about that person's teen-affirming plans.

PART 3: HELPING YOUR TEEN MAKE THE RIGHT CHOICES

Session 9
Where to Begin: A Christian Worldview

1. Optional Opener

If time allows and your group is open to having a little fun, try the following activity. Form two teams. Team 1 pretends that it's living in the England of Shakespeare's time. Team 2 lives in the future in a high-tech U.S. colony on Mars. Give people a few moments to get into the mind-sets of their places and eras.

Now read the following fictional newspaper headlines and let teams react as the people they're pretending to be.
- "Smallpox Vaccine Invented"
- "Killer Asteroid on Collision Course with Earth"
- "Queen Visits Local Rugby Match"
- "Scientists Say Sunlight Causes Cancer"
- "*Star Wars* Sequel Tops Box Office"

Then ask:

How did your view of the world affect your perception of these headlines?

If you're a Christian, what's one way in which your view of the world affects your everyday life?

What's one way in which your teen's worldview influences his or her choices?

2. Startup

To encourage brief discussion of the chapter introduction, ask:

Do you think most teenagers would agree with the student in this story? Why or why not?

How would you define the phrase "Christian worldview"?

If group members haven't read the "Startup" and "Survey" sections, don't take the time to do so now. Instead, go directly to the "Scripture" section.

3. Survey

If group members have completed this multiple-choice feature on their own, they may have a few answers—humorous or serious—to share. Let a few volunteers do so. Then ask:

Which of the following comes to mind when I say, "Christian world-view"?

a. Egghead professors

b. Thought police

c. Sound doctrine

d. Other (explain)

4. Scripture

If your group is large, form pairs or teams to discuss the answers participants came up with during the week. Then regather the whole group and let spokespersons summarize the teams' findings. For groups who haven't done the homework, allow more time to read and discuss the Bible passages in the book.

Whether or not people have prepared, you might find it useful to ask these follow-up questions:

So far, where has your teen gotten most of his input on what it means to "think like a Christian"—directly from the Bible, from church, from a Christian school, or from you?

Would you say your teen has developed the kind of worldview represented in these verses? If not, what are the main gaps you'd like to see filled?

5. Strategies

Groups who haven't read the advice article will need time to become familiar with its content. You can summarize it, read it aloud, let volunteers take turns reading it, or have everyone read it silently.

Once people are up to speed, try asking questions like these:

Do you think having a Christian worldview is more a matter of the head or the heart? Why?

Do you feel qualified to address this subject with your teen? If not, what kind of help would you need?

If you tried to convey one point from this article to your teen each month, which three would you choose first?

6. Steps to Take

To make the application as personal as possible, and to give everyone a chance to talk, form pairs or teams if your group has more than four members. If participants have worked through this section on their own, spend as much time as you can letting them share their responses. Otherwise, have people work through selected questions (we'd suggest numbers 1, 5, and 6) now.

If time allows, follow up by encouraging people to use books like the following to help their teens develop a Christian worldview.

My Truth, Your Truth, Whose Truth? By Randy Petersen (Focus on the Family/Tyndale)

Answers to Tough Questions by Josh McDowell and Don Stewart (Thomas Nelson)

Life on the Edge by Dr. James Dobson (Word)

If I Could Ask God One Question by Greg Johnson (Bethany House)

Session 10
Guiding Your Teen Toward Faith-Affirming Friendships

1. Optional Opener
If time allows and your group is open to having a little fun, try the following activity. You'll need a spoon for each group member, plenty of peanuts, and some open space.

Form pairs. Give each person a spoon; give each pair a peanut. Each pair is to use its spoon to carry its peanut from the middle of the room to the side. The catch: Each partner is trying to get to a different side.

Participants may touch spoon to spoon or spoon to peanut, but no other contact is allowed. Let them struggle for a couple of minutes before calling a halt to the contest. Then ask:

Did any of the pairs win this game? Why or why not?

How is this like a friendship between two people who don't share the same values?

Do you think your teen sees any problem with having a close friendship or romantic relationship with a non-Christian? How do you know?

2. Startup
To encourage brief discussion of the chapter introduction, ask:

Which of these two stories do you think is more unusual? Why?
Does it surprise you to know that parents have such an influence in their teens' lives? Why or why not?

If group members haven't read the "Startup" and "Survey" sections, don't take the time to do so now. Instead, go directly to the "Scripture" section.

3. Survey

If group members have completed this multiple-choice feature on their own, they may have a few answers—humorous or serious—to share. Let a few volunteers do so. Then ask:

When it comes to screening your teen's friends, how does your approach compare to the one your parents took with *your* friends? Are you satisfied with the results?

4. Scripture

If your group is large, form pairs or teams to discuss the answers participants came up with during the week. Then regather the whole group and let spokespersons summarize the teams' findings. For groups who haven't done the homework, allow more time to read and discuss the Bible passages in the book.

Follow up with these questions if time allows:

"What does a believer have in common with an unbeliever?" How would you answer this question from 2 Corinthians 6:15?

How does your answer help to define how your teen should relate to non-Christians?

5. Strategies

Groups who haven't read the advice article will need time to become familiar with its content. You can summarize it, read it aloud, let volunteers take turns reading it, or have everyone read it silently.

Once people are up to speed, try asking questions like these:

Which of Jim Weidmann's ideas do you think are worth adopting?

What different approaches would you want to take?

How far would you go to separate your teen from a friend or romantic partner you believed was a bad influence on him or her?

6. Steps to Take

To make the application as personal as possible, and to give everyone a chance to talk, form pairs or teams if your group has more than four members. If participants have worked through this section on their own, spend as much time as you can letting them share their responses. Otherwise, have people work through selected questions (we'd suggest numbers 2, 4, 5, and 7) now.

If possible, follow up with questions like these:

If you could give your teen only one piece of advice on friendship, what would it be?

How do you think your teen would respond to that advice? Why?
Without naming names, is there a friend, girlfriend, or boyfriend of your teen that we can pray for?

If participants answer affirmatively, spend some time praying together for those young people. Also encourage group members to pray for wisdom in monitoring their teens' friendships, and that their teens will be a positive influence on peers.

Session 11
Teaching Your Teen Media Discernment

1. Optional Opener
Bring a bagful of music CDs in their cases, and some small prizes. Have a volunteer come to the front.

Call out the title of one of the CDs in the bag. The volunteer closes his eyes and reaches into the bag; if he pulls out the CD you've named, he gets a prize. If not, he has to tell the group about a time when he and his teen clashed over an entertainment choice. As time allows, let a few other volunteers go through the same process.

Then ask the group:

If you had to go into a store and pick out the CDs and DVDs your teen is into these days, could you do it?

Why is it important to help our teens choose entertainment with their eyes and ears open?

2. Startup
To encourage brief discussion of the chapter introduction, ask:

What do you think might have gone wrong in Larry's case?

What do you think Larry would say to us if he were here today?

If group members haven't read the "Startup" and "Survey" sections, don't take the time to do so now. Instead, go directly to the "Scripture" section.

3. Survey
If group members have completed this multiple-choice feature on their own, they

may have a few answers—humorous or serious—to share. Let a few volunteers do so. Then ask:

Does your teen fit any of these stereotypes?

a. The kid who's always driving his parents crazy by listening to loud music

b. The kid who's oblivious to his surroundings because he's always wearing headphones

c. The kid who's addicted to violent video games or computer games

d. The kid who's always glued to the TV screen

e. The kid who wants to see every slasher movie and teen sex comedy

If not, what is your teen's attitude toward media?

4. Scripture

If your group is large, form pairs or teams to discuss the answers participants came up with during the week. Then regather the whole group and let spokespersons summarize the teams' findings. For groups who haven't done the homework, allow more time to read and discuss the Bible passages in the book.

Whether or not people have prepared, you might find it useful to ask these follow-up questions:

What would you say to a teen who says, "Hey, don't take this so seriously; it's only entertainment"?

On a scale of 1 to 10 (10 highest), how successful have you been in applying biblical standards to your own media choices?

Do you think this has influenced your teen? If so, how?

5. Strategies

Groups who haven't read the advice article will need time to become familiar with its content. You can summarize it, read it aloud, let volunteers take turns reading it, or have everyone read it silently.

Once people are up to speed, try asking questions like these:

Have you tried any of these approaches already? If so, how did they work out?

What one action described in this article probably would make the most difference in your teen's media choices?

What does it mean to "treasure hunt" while making media choices? What's one media treasure your family has found?

6. Steps to Take

To make the application as personal as possible, and to give everyone a chance to talk, form pairs or teams if your group has more than four members. If participants have worked through this section on their own, spend as much time as you can letting them share their responses. Otherwise, have people work through selected questions (we'd suggest numbers 2, 3, and 5) now.

If possible, follow up with questions like these:

In which of the following areas do you think your teen is making the best choices right now: music, movies, TV, video games, or the Internet?

How could you affirm those good choices this week?

If you're concerned about some of your teen's media choices, could writing a "Family Constitution for Acceptable Media" together be a nonthreatening way to bring up the subject? Or would you suggest a different approach?

To close, encourage pairs or teams to pray for the success of group members' efforts to help their teens make better media choices.

Session 12
When You and Your Teen Disagree

1. Optional Opener

If time allows and your group is open to having a little fun, try the following activity. You'll need some temporary tattoos, the kind children apply with water, often available in toy stores or where stickers or candy are sold. You'll need some washcloths and water, too.

Let people pick out tattoos as they come in. Then have them apply the designs to the backs of their hands, using washcloths and water, and show them off to the group.

Then ask:

What would you do if your teen came home with a tattoo—not a temporary one, but a permanent one?

How about body piercing? Would you accept a pierced ear, but not a pierced eyebrow? What if it were your son, not your daughter?

What are some other "fashion statements" that cause conflict between parents and teens?

Why is it important for a spiritual mentor to know how to handle parent-teen conflict?

2. Startup

To encourage brief discussion of the chapter introduction, ask:

How would you handle the case of the 16-year-old daughter?

Is there anything in Raymond's story that you can relate to? If so, what?

If group members haven't read the "Startup" and "Survey" sections, don't take the time to do so now. Instead, go directly to the "Scripture" section.

3. Survey

If group members have completed this multiple-choice feature on their own, they may have a few answers—humorous or serious—to share. Let a few volunteers do so. Then ask:

Is it normal for parents and teens to be in conflict? Why or why not?

Parent-teen conflict is often used as raw material for humor. When it happens in your family, though, are you able to keep a sense of humor about it? Why or why not?

4. Scripture

If your group is large, form pairs or teams to discuss the answers participants came up with during the week. Then regather the whole group and let spokespersons summarize the teams' findings. For groups who haven't done the homework, allow more time to read and discuss the Bible passages in the book.

Whether or not people have prepared, you might find it useful to ask these follow-up questions:

Do any of these Bible passages remind you of a situation you've faced recently?

If so, how might that situation have turned out differently if you'd followed the advice in these scriptures?

5. Strategies

Groups who haven't read the advice article will need time to become familiar with its content. You can summarize it, read it aloud, let volunteers take turns reading it, or have everyone read it silently.

Once people are up to speed, ask:

What's your reaction to each of the following quotes from the article?
- **"Recognize that body piercings are fads—and fads die out."**
- **"I'd rather have my kid come home with hair that makes me cringe than to rebel through the use of drugs."**

- "Every family has to choose its own issues that are worth fighting over."
- "Discernment is the ultimate goal in dealing with these issues. . . . We must use these situations to help them . . . make wise choices on their own."

6. Steps to Take

To make the application as personal as possible, and to give everyone a chance to talk, form pairs or teams if your group has more than four members. If participants have worked through this section on their own, spend as much time as you can letting them share their responses. If people haven't prepared, have them work through selected exercises (we'd suggest numbers 5, 6, and 7) now.

If time allows, follow up with questions like these:

Does mentoring your teen spiritually require getting rid of all conflict between the two of you? Why or why not?

How could some kinds of conflict *contribute* to spiritually training your teen?

What's one thing you've learned from this course that could help your teen make better choices?

How can we keep in touch to encourage each other?

Consider participants' suggestions on how to stay in contact. Ideas might include exchanging phone numbers and e-mail addresses if you haven't already done so, meeting again in a couple of months for an update, or organizing a prayer chain.

To close, have pairs or teams pray for each other. If possible, be available after the meeting to hear participants' concerns and to thank them for contributing to the success of your group.

PART 4: DISCIPLING DAY BY DAY

Session 13
Creating an "Eager Learner" Attitude

1. Optional Opener

If time allows and your group is open to having a little fun, try the following activity. You'll need as many kinds of "sticks" as you can find—twigs, Popsicle sticks, Pixy Stix, pick-up sticks, drum sticks, glue sticks, turkey drum sticks, etc.

Form a team for each type of stick you've brought. Explain that teams are going to compete to see which team can start a fire first by rubbing its sticks together. When you say "Go," participants have 30 seconds to get their sticks to ignite.

Chances are very slim that anyone's sticks will burst into flame. Ask:

Why didn't this work?

How is this like trying to start a spiritual fire in your teenager?

What do you think is the most important requirement for raising a teen who's "on fire" for the Lord?

2. Startup

To encourage brief discussion of the chapter introduction, ask:

Have you known anyone like Steven? Did that person ever make a similar turnaround? If so, how?

If group members haven't read the "Startup" and "Survey" sections, don't take the time to do so now. Instead, go directly to the "Scripture" section.

3. Survey

If group members have completed this multiple-choice feature on their own, they may have a few answers—humorous or serious—to share. Let a few volunteers do so. Then ask:

Is it realistic to expect any teenager to be an "eager learner" when it comes to spiritual things? If not, what's the best a parent should hope for?

4. Scripture

If your group is large, form pairs or teams to discuss the answers participants came up with during the week. Then regather the whole group and let spokespersons summarize the teams' findings. For groups who haven't done the homework, allow more time to read and discuss the Bible passages in the book.

Whether or not people have prepared, you might find it useful to ask these follow-up questions:

Do you think Jesus met people's needs only so that they would make spiritual progress? Why or why not?

Which of these biblical cases comes closest to echoing a need your teen might have? On a scale of 1 to 10 (10 highest), how adequate do you feel to meet that need? What role would you like God to play in that process?

5. Strategies

Groups who haven't read the advice article will need time to become familiar with its content. You can summarize it, read it aloud, let volunteers take turns reading it, or have everyone read it silently.

Once people are up to speed, try asking questions like these:

Which one of these seven factors might have helped most with your spiritual growth as a teenager? Why?

Which one might make the biggest difference for your teenager today?

6. Steps to Take

To make the application as personal as possible, and to give everyone a chance to talk, form pairs or teams if your group has more than four members. If participants have worked through this section on their own, spend as much time as you can letting them share their responses. Otherwise, have people work through selected questions (we'd suggest choosing any three of the first seven, plus question 8) now.

If time allows, follow up with questions like these:

Do you feel ready to follow through on any of the suggestions in this chapter?

If so, which one needs to be your top priority?

If not, what would help you feel more ready?

To close, encourage pairs or teams to pray for the success of group members' plans to help their teens become eager learners.

Session 14
Ideas for Raising a Faithful Follower

1. Optional Opener

If you have time and your group doesn't mind having a little fun, start off with a Discipleship Makeover.

Bring costume items that might normally show up in a church Christmas pageant—bathrobes, towels and headbands for Mideastern headgear, pieces of rope for belts, sandals, shepherd's crooks, fake beards, wigs, etc. Form two teams; give each team a supply of clothing and props. Each team should choose a person to dress up as a "disciple."

After a few minutes, compare the results of the makeovers. Pick a winner if you like. Then ask:

What does a disciple look like?

If clothes don't make the disciple, what does?

Is it possible to turn your teen into a disciple of Jesus? If not, what's the point of "discipling" him or her?

2. Startup

To encourage brief discussion of the chapter introduction, ask:

How would you answer the question of what your "one thing" is right now?

If helping your teen follow Christ became your "one thing," what other things might have to go on the back burner?

If group members haven't read the "Startup" and "Survey" sections, don't take the time to do so now. Instead, go directly to the "Scripture" section.

3. Survey

If group members have completed this multiple-choice feature on their own, they may have a few answers—humorous or serious—to share. Let a few volunteers do so. Then ask:

If you had to sum up in one word your approach to discipling your teen so far, what would it be? Why?

4. Scripture

If your group is large, form pairs or teams to discuss the answers participants came up with during the week. Then regather the whole group and let spokespersons summarize the teams' findings. For groups who haven't done the homework, allow more time to read and discuss the Bible passages in the book.

Whether or not people have prepared, you might find it useful to ask these follow-up questions:

Do you see yourself as your teen's "spiritual parent"? Why or why not?

Which of the following aspects of discipling seems most important to your teen's spiritual development right now: sharpening each other, carrying each other's burdens, confession, or role modeling? Why?

5. Strategies

Groups who haven't read the advice article will need time to become familiar with its content. You can summarize it, read it aloud, let volunteers take turns reading it, or have everyone read it silently.

Once people are up to speed, you may find they're overwhelmed by the 12 ideas—especially if they think parents are supposed to implement all of them. Explain that these 12 ideas are like tools in a toolbox—to be used as needed. Then ask:

Which of these suggestions are "how-tos" and which are "what-tos"? How could the concept of "teachable moments" help you apply some of the other ideas?

Which idea would be easiest to work into your routine this week?

6. Steps to Take

To make the application as personal as possible, and to give everyone a chance to talk, form pairs or teams if your group has more than four members. If participants have worked through this section on their own, spend as much time as you can letting them share their responses. Otherwise, have people work through selected questions (we'd suggest picking any three) now.

If possible, follow up with questions like these:

Do any of these stories remind you of experiences you had growing up? If so, how did those experiences contribute to your desire to follow Jesus?

What do these stories have in common?

How do you suppose the parents involved in these stories feel about those experiences now?

To close, encourage pairs or teams to pray for the success of group members' efforts to disciple their teens.

Session 15
Never Quit on a Child

1. Optional Opener

If time allows and your group likes to have fun, have a contest to see who can go the longest at one of the following activities:

- Not breathing
- Doing push-ups
- Reciting a Bible passage of your choosing
- Eating jalapeño peppers

After your contest, congratulate any winners. Then ask:

How did you know when it was time to quit?

When it comes to being your teen's spiritual mentor, how do you know when it's time to quit?

Is it ever time to "give up" on your teen? Why or why not?

2. Startup

To encourage brief discussion of the chapter introduction, ask:

When you hear the word "relentless," what do you think of?

To "relent" means to surrender. What might a parent of a teen be tempted to surrender to?

If group members haven't read the "Startup" and "Survey" sections, don't take the time to do so now. Instead, go directly to the "Scripture" section.

3. Survey

If group members have completed this multiple-choice feature on their own, they may have a few answers—humorous or serious—to share. Let a few volunteers do so. Then ask:

If we were going to start an organization called the Society of Parents Who Have Been Tempted to Give Up on Their Kids (SPWHBTGUTK), what would be the membership requirements?

What would we do at our meetings?

What would be our goal?

4. Scripture

If your group is large, form pairs or teams to discuss the answers participants came up with during the week. Then regather the whole group and let spokespersons summarize the teams' findings. For groups who haven't done the homework, allow more time to read and discuss the Bible passages in the book.

Whether or not people have prepared, you might find it useful to ask these follow-up questions:

Does God just tell us not to give up, or does He give us resources to help us keep going?

What resources are implied in these scriptures and in other Bible passages you may have read?

5. Strategies

Groups who haven't read the advice article will need time to become familiar with its content. You can summarize it, read it aloud, let volunteers take turns reading it, or have everyone read it silently.

Once people are up to speed, try asking questions like these:

What did you think of Amanda's story? If you were her parents, what might you have done differently?

Which of the "Seven Habits of Highly Relentless Parents" seems most crucial to you?

What's one you've tried to practice and from which you've seen positive results?

6. Steps to Take

To make the application as personal as possible, and to give everyone a chance to talk, form pairs or teams if your group has more than four members. If participants have worked through this section on their own, spend as much time as you can letting them share their responses. If people haven't prepared, have them work through selected exercises (we'd suggest numbers 1, 2, and 7) now.

If time allows, follow up with questions like these:

What's one thing this discussion has helped you appreciate about the relationship you have with your teenager?

What gives you the most hope that things can get even better?

How can we keep encouraging you not to give up on your teen?

Session 16
Learning to Let Go

1. Optional Opener

If time allows and your group is open to having a little fun, try the following activity. You'll need a rope that's at least 10 feet long, plus two volunteers.

Warn your volunteers in advance to dress for a tug-of-war. If possible, stage it outside on grass or sand. Divide the group in half, with each volunteer representing half the group. Tell everyone that at some point during the contest you'll be yelling, "Let go!" When that happens, the opponents must release the rope immediately. Anyone who falls down loses the game for his or her side.

Start the tug-of-war, making sure both participants are really pulling. Then say, "Let go!" Chances are that the players will be caught off balance, even if no one actually falls.

Then ask:

How did knowing you would have to let go affect your pulling?

How is raising a teenager like a tug-of-war?

Is it better to "let go" of a teenager all at once, or a little at a time? Why?

When you think about having to "let go" of your teen someday, how do you feel?

2. Startup

To encourage brief discussion of the chapter introduction, ask:

Which of these scenarios strikes the most fear into your heart? Why?

Do you think your teen would be ready to handle these situations today? Why or why not?

If group members haven't read the "Startup" and "Survey" sections, don't take the time to do so now. Instead, go directly to the "Scripture" section.

3. Survey

If group members have completed this multiple-choice feature on their own, they may have a few answers—humorous or serious—to share. Let a few volunteers do so. Then ask:

Who seems more eager to cut the apron strings at your house—you or your teen?

On a scale of 1 to 10 (10 highest), how confident are you that your teen will be spiritually ready for "independence day" when the time comes? Why?

4. Scripture

If your group is large, form pairs or teams to discuss the answers participants came up with during the week. Then regather the whole group and let spokespersons summarize the teams' findings. For groups who haven't done the homework, allow more time to read and discuss the Bible passages in the book.

Whether or not people have prepared, you might find it useful to ask these follow-up questions:

Jesus and Elisha both had a strong sense of purpose, a belief that God had a job for them to do. How would that belief help a young person who's on the verge of adulthood?

How can a parent help a teen develop such a sense of spiritual purpose?

5. Strategies

Groups who haven't read the advice article will need time to become familiar with its content. You can summarize it, read it aloud, let volunteers take turns reading it, or have everyone read it silently.

Once people are up to speed, try asking questions like these:

After reading this article, do you feel you've been giving your teen too much freedom, too little, or about the right amount?

Was there anything about your own experience as a young adult that reinforces what was said here? If so, what was it?

If you could add one "Prep Point" of your own, what would it be?

6. Steps to Take

To make the application as personal as possible, and to give everyone a chance to talk, form pairs or teams if your group has more than four members. If participants have worked through this section on their own, spend as much time as you can letting them share their responses. If people haven't prepared, have them work through selected exercises (we'd suggest numbers 1, 4, and 5) now.

If time allows, follow up with questions like these:

During the next six months, where do you want to concentrate your efforts in preparing your teen for "letting go"?

What three things do you most want to remember from this course?

How can we keep in touch to encourage each other?

Consider participants' suggestions on how to stay in contact. Ideas might include exchanging phone numbers and e-mail addresses if you haven't already done so, meeting again in a couple of months for an update, or organizing a prayer chain.

To close, have pairs or teams pray for each other. If possible, be available after the meeting to hear participants' concerns and to thank them for contributing to the success of your group.

Notes

Chapter 1
1. James C. Dobson, *Home with a Heart* (Wheaton, Ill.: Tyndale, 1996), p. 154.

Chapter 4
1. From the "Walk Away" Web site sponsored by the Institute for First Amendment Studies.

Chapter 7
1. James C. Dobson, *Complete Marriage and Family Home Reference Guide* (Wheaton, Ill.: Tyndale, 2000), p. 226.

Chapter 8
1. Based on Joe White, *What Kids Wish Parents Knew About Parenting* (Sisters, Oreg.: Questar, 1988), pp. 176-78.

Chapter 10
1. "Teenagers and Their Relationships," Barna Research Group, July 8, 1998.
2. Ibid.

Chapter 11
1. Newton Minow, *How Vast the Wasteland Now?* (New York: Gannett Foundation Media Center, 1991) (www.KSU.edu/humec/kulaw.htm).

Chapter 12
1. Dr. Allen Johnson, "Mom, I Want a Tattoo," *Christian Parenting Today,* July/August 1998 (www.christianitytoday.com).

Chapter 14
1. Adapted from Manfred Koehler, "Window to the World," *Single-Parent Family* (www.family.org).

Dear Friend,

Being a dad is a great privilege. It's been the most exciting, overwhelming and unforgettable experience that's ever happened to me! If you've also had the privilege of parenting, I'm sure you feel the same way.

But I know another feeling most of us moms and dads have: "Who can I turn to that understands what I'm dealing with?"

That's why Focus on Your Child was launched by Focus on the Family. We're here to help you find answers and enjoy the journey of raising your kids. It's never been easier to find the help and encouragement you've been looking for.

I invite you to visit our Web site at **www.focusonyourchild.com** and see for yourself just how much great parenting insight is waiting there for you to explore. And while you're there, you can sign up for a complimentary membership that includes many "parenting perks," including audio journals and newsletters based on the ages of your children.

Parenting is an adventure — let us help you enjoy the journey!

Sincerely,

Leon Lowman, Jr.
Senior Director, Focus on Your Child

Give Your Teens
GUIDANCE

Parents' Guide to the
Spiritual Mentoring of Teens

The teen years are critical to developing adult children who know, love and serve the Lord. This guide offers solid, proven advice and techniques that will enable you to succeed in the changing parent-teen relationship. It will also equip you to ignite a passion in your teens to become wholehearted disciples. Hardcover.

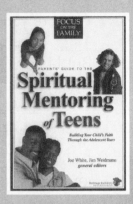

Fuel

Fuel helps busy teens connect with their parents. Youth expert Joe White has put together powerful 10-minute devotions from the New Testament for you to share. It's fun, fast and filled with memorable stories, discussion starters and lifeline applications — all designed to get parents and teens talking. Paperback.

Wired by God

Wired by God is a unique parent/teen book and interactive CD set designed to help teens figure out the possibilities for their futures. Filled with fun, interesting ways to pinpoint gifts, talents, personality traits and more, this set will spark great conversations to bring parents and teens closer. Hardcover with CD.